LITTLE GIRL,

B G

GOD

LORRIE LOCKHART

Authenticity Book House
c/o Proven Way Ministries
The Hope Center
2001 W. Plano Parkway, Suite 3422
Plano, TX 75075

Little Girl, Big God
Copyright © 2016 by Lorrie Lockhart

ISBN: 978-1-943004-05-8 (p)

All Scripture quotations, unless otherwise indicated, are taken from the New American Standard Bible, © Copyright 1960, 1962, and 1995 by the Lockman Foundation. Used by permission.

Scripture quotations marked ESV are taken from The Holy Bible: English Standard Version, copyright 2001, Wheaton: Good News Publishers. Used by permission. All rights reserved.

Because of the dynamic nature of the Internet, any web addresses or links contained in this book may have changed since publication and may no longer be valid.

Published by Authenticity Book House
Printed in the United States of America
10 9 8 7 6 5 4 3 2 1

AUTHENTICITY
BOOK HOUSE

I want to dedicate this book to my four beautiful, wonderful daughters,

Leah Gehret, Elizabeth Gregory,
Frances Geiger Joslin and Alice Schaible.

They have been my editors, my critics, and my encouragers.

They and their families are a constant source of joy and blessing.

Table of Contents

Introduction

This autobiography should be considered a companion to my husband's book, *A Missionary's Journal*, by Austin Lockhart, though it begins about twenty years earlier. I sincerely believe God has a plan for each of our lives, and He begins early preparing us for His plan. This is my story of how God led me from an early age to be His servant. I am deeply grateful for His love and care, His patience and perseverance in molding me and in using me for His glory.

I also want to express gratitude to my Mom. Though she only had a sixth-grade education, she was an exceptionally wise and caring woman. Once Mom surrendered her life to Christ, she followed Him wholeheartedly, ignoring friends who tried to persuade her otherwise. When some missionary friends of ours were killed in New Guinea, some said, "Audy and Lorrie could get killed too! You should tell them to come home!"

"No," she answered, "They could just as easily be killed in a car crash or something else here at home. They are safer where God wants them."

She was always a great supporter, encourager, and prayer warrior.

As far as I know, Daddy never accepted Jesus as his Savior, though many people tried to convince him of his need. Yet in many ways he was a good father. He was determined that all of us get a good education and worked hard to provide for us, though he did abandon the whole family for a time. He grieved over losing his family and rejoiced when all of us eventually forgave him. He tried reconciling with Mom a few times, but she had suffered too much and didn't think it would work. Later in life he married again and moved to Virginia where we visited as often as we could. I inherited and learned a great deal from my father.

I am grateful to all the wonderful schools I attended. All of them have grown in the intervening years. Some have different names now and have expanded their programs. But all are still active in providing good educations.

Appalachian Bible College is now, of course, a much bigger school, but it still teaches the truths of God's Word. Their motto is "Life is for service," and each year they emphasize a different aspect of servanthood.

Grace Gospel Church epitomizes what a home church should be. They have prayed, encouraged, given, befriended, fed us, and hundreds of other things, as well as supported us financially. We were truly blessed to have them as our sending church. We were also thankful for all the other churches and individuals who supported, prayed consistently for us and the people of New Guinea, and helped us in more ways than I can innumerate.

The Unevangelized Fields Mission (Crossworld) is a godly, caring, helpful, and wise mission board. God certainly led us to the right board for our missionary service.

It is my fervent prayer that this book will bring glory to God and that He will use it in the lives of all who read it. God has given me a very fulfilling and happy life. Praise His name!

The Light

Like a candle faintly beaming,
Swaying, flickering,
Struggling on,
Lest the darkness overcome it
E'er it's appointed task was done.

Just a dim light in the distance,
But it pointed out the way,
And it seemed to hold the promise,
"Greater light you'll see someday."

So it was, as life continued
And I learned the way of love,
That the light grew ever brighter,
Giving guidance from above.

Lorrie Lockhart

1

Hollybush

"Call to Me and I will answer you, and I will tell you great
and mighty things I didn't which you do not know."

JEREMIAH 33:3

I had traveled by bus all night and was bone tired, but now I was
in a car with a strange man who was driving much too fast. I soon
became very alert. It was dark outside, but I could see the forms of
buildings and trees flying by as if on an out-of-control conveyer belt.
The driver increased his speed. My mind raced, *What am I going I
do? I need to get out of this car!* I tried to stay calm. I didn't want to
anger him. I did my best to talk to him about God, but he ignored
me and kept driving so fast that it would have been impossible to
jump out of the car. I prayed desperately for God to help me out of
this predicament that I had foolishly gotten myself into. *Maybe when
he slows down for a curve, I could jump out. Lord help me!*

Questions plagued my thoughts. Was this going to be the end of
my plans to become a missionary? God had helped me all along the
way, providing guidance, finances, and all that was needed through

all those years of education. Was it now going to end because of this one foolish decision? Was my life itself going to end?

❖ ❖ ❖

I first heard the gospel and met my first missionary as an eight-year-old child at my school in rural Kentucky. The Hollybush schoolhouse was small like most schoolhouses in our area of the Kentucky Mountains. It had once been painted white but now looked closer to gray, and the paint was peeling. Inside sat approximately forty students, ranging in age from five to fifteen. They were all in the "Big Room" for this was a special day. Mr. Clayton Hull, a tall man with brown eyes and dark hair, stood in front telling a Bible story.

He was a missionary who traveled several miles on horseback to tell us this story and to invite us to memorize Bible verses for various rewards. Five verses won a Gospel of John; twenty-five verses from the Gospel of John won a New Testament. The ultimate prize was a week at Camp Nathanael, which required memorizing a total of 250 Bible verses and reciting them to the Bible teacher.

I don't remember the story Mr. Hull told that day, but I know I accepted one of the slips of paper on which the first five verses were printed. It was time for recess, and those who accepted the papers spent the time studying. When the bell rang, we returned to our classes. The first five grades studied in the Big Room and sixth, seventh, and eighth in the smaller room. I was in the Little Room, for I was in the sixth grade.

I, Lorrie (Ellora is my given name) Caudill, started school when I was four years old. There were no rules in 1937 about how early a child could start. It was up to the parents and the willingness of the teacher to accept them. Mom sent all six of her children at age four. My brother, Chad, was the only child the teachers refused. He wouldn't sit still. There was no kindergarten or pre-school available, so I started with the first grade. When I came back the next year for second grade, I was able to read the second grade reader all the way through, so I was moved to third grade. Therefore, when Mr. Hull came in 1941, I was only eight years old but in the sixth grade. I was very small for my age, so I looked even younger.

When Mr. Hull returned two weeks later, my sister Christine and I, along with a few others, said the five verses and received our little Gospel of John booklet. But the next time he returned, Christine and I could say only seven or eight of the twenty-five verses required from the Gospel of John, and we didn't say them very well. We felt terrible when he told us we would need to do better next time. All the other students had given up completely, but Christine and I determined to learn all twenty-five verses and to say them well the next time.

At the end of the two weeks we were well-prepared, but we were two very disappointed little girls when Mr. Hull didn't return. Looking back years later, I understand that it was a long journey. He could only have made a few visits before the weather turned cold and the roads became muddy or frozen. He had only two little girls saying the verses, and not very well at that. How could he know of the yearning of our hearts or of our mother's promise?

My Mom, Madge Huff Caudill, had known about Camp Nathanael for a few years since its location was only about twenty miles from our home. At one time she had met its founder, Garland Franklin, and believed that he was doing a good thing in making this opportunity to go to camp available for the children of our area. She determined that if any of her children wanted to go, she would help them all she could, regardless of the difficulties. So, when missionaries started coming to our school, she told us, "If you learn the Bible verses, I'll see to it that you go to camp." But that year it had to be put aside.

❖ ❖ ❖

My family consisted of my parents, Henry C. and Madge Caudill, and children in order of birth: Ivallean, Arlene, me, Christine, and the youngest, a boy named Chad. Priscilla came along later. Home was a happy place with lots of joking, laughing, and singing. We lived in a big ten-room, slate blue house about two miles from the Hollybush School.

We each had our own room. The girls slept upstairs. Chad was only two-and-a-half and slept downstairs near Mom and Dad. There was a large kitchen, dining room, living room, and three bedrooms on the first floor. It had a large porch across the front and partway on the right side, leading to the kitchen door. This was an unusually big house for Hollybush, and very few houses were painted. But Daddy was always one who loved to experiment and explore new and different things.

We hadn't lived in the large house very long. The original house consisted of only three rooms. The entrance was into the middle room which contained two full-sized beds where all the children slept, two to a bed. It had the only fireplace in the whole house and later became the living room. To the left of the entrance was the kitchen and eating area. I remember a big round table in front of a large window. The room on the right was Mom and Dad's room.

I was about five years old when Daddy decided to rebuild. While our home was being renovated, we moved into a one-room place owned by Daddy's parents. Fortunately it was a spacious room—big enough to allow for three full-sized beds on the right side of the room. At the back of the room and slightly to the left sat the cooking stove and an area for stacked firewood and buckets of coal. A few cupboards to the left of the stove held dishes and needed supplies. A long table stood in the center of the room, and a fireplace near the center of the left wall kept us warm. It was crowded but manageable. We lived there several months.

The men Daddy hired to build the house were a father and son team. Tom, the father, was very hump-backed—bent over so far that he had to turn his whole body to look up at you. With his thin, grey, unruly hair and long, bony fingers, he looked much like Scrooge from *The Christmas Carol* by Charles Dickens. His son was cross-eyed and had thin, straight, brown hair. Both were missing several teeth, and they chewed tobacco that stained the few remaining ones. But they really knew how to build houses. They slept in the old/new house, but took all their meals with us. It kept Mom really busy feeding everyone, but Tom and his son kept us entertained with stories of houses they built, people they knew, and situations they encountered. We children loved having them there.

Just about the time the new house was finished and we started to move back in, my brother, Chad, was born. Daddy's parents lived only about a half mile down the road from us, so Grandma Caudill had always helped Mom with the birth of her children, though she had no formal training, except the mentoring of other self taught midwives called "Granny Women."

Mom's first child presented breach, and Grandma didn't know how to handle that. Lilly Ann died about an hour after birth. Mom's third child, her first son, Jarrel Dean, was born healthy, but died at five months old because of simple diarrhea. No one understood how to treat it, and doctors were too far away. It was not uncommon in those days to lose two or three children, or more, but that fact didn't lessen the pain for the family. More than fifty years later, Mom would tear-up when she talked about her babies who didn't have a chance to grow up.

This time though Chad Rondal was born healthy and thriving. My sister Ivallean (Ivy), though only twelve years old, assisted Grandma. Ivy decided then and there that she wanted to deliver babies, but with a big difference—she would get lots of training.

❖ ❖ ❖

Our house and yard were only a small part of a fifteen-acre farm. There was a large garden to the right of the house where we raised lots of vegetables. Daddy plowed the ground in the spring. Mom would then do the planting and hoeing, with a little help from her children. A large strawberry patch in the center of the garden produced sweet juicy fruit, smaller than the strawberries we see today, but much more flavorful. At the lower edge of the garden a golden delicious apple tree, its branches often drooping with abundant fruit, gave us the best tasting apples I have ever eaten.

Corn grew high on the hill behind our house in a huge field. It had to be hoed twice each season. It was the children's job to carry cold drinking water up to the workers. Beans were usually planted with the corn. As the corn grew upward, the bean vines wound around the stalks and produced beans before the corn matured. We wore long sleeves when picking the beans to prevent the blades of the corn from cutting our arms. We then carried the beans down the hill in large white sacks. We spent hours stringing the beans for drying or breaking them for canning. Sometimes we traded beans for other supplies. In early fall, we harvested the corn and brought it down to the barn by mule and sled. It was usually enough to feed the cows and mules until the next year's crop was harvested.

To the left of the house stood a barn and a shed for farm equipment, coal, and chopped wood.

Coal for cooking and warmth in winter was "dug" from the "coal bank" up on the hill in back of our garden. Daddy usually brought the coal down using a sled and mule. Two or three loads would last through the winter.

We had many fruit trees on our property—peach, mulberry, and several types of apple. We even had walnuts, the long shaped ones, harder to crack than the English variety. A few years before we moved away from the farm, Daddy planted a large orchard of several varieties of apples and peaches. Sadly, the trees were only beginning to produce fruit when we moved, so we never got to enjoy all those new varieties.

Daddy also had several bee hives which he "robbed" once or twice a year, bringing wash tubs full of honey to the house! As soon as he sat the tub on the porch floor, we eagerly started eating. We loved chewing on the honeycomb even though sometimes a few live bees were on the combs. We had to be careful. Of course, Mom set limits on how much honey we could eat.

Almost everyone on Hollybush Creek owned a horse or mule, or both. It was necessary for plowing the fields, hauling things, and for riding to the grocery store or the post office, which sometimes was the same place. Actually, though we did a lot of walking, most long distances required horseback riding. I loved riding. Sometimes we rode over to Caney Creek to visit our grandparents, Ma and Pa Hutt, Mom's parents.

Once when Chad was a baby, Mom, Chad, Christine, and I made that trip. Mom rode in the saddle with Chad in front of her, and Chris and I held on behind. We spent the night and started home the next day, even though it was bitter cold with some snow on the ground. About two miles from home, our horse got frightened at something and threw us off right into a mud puddle!

Somehow he managed to kick Mom just below her eye, which later became very black. Thankfully, a friend came along at the right time and brought the horse back. We got back on, but we were quite shaken, wet, and miserable. I remember crying because I was so cold by the time we got home. Mom quickly stirred up the fire, and soon we were warm, and no one suffered any permanent damage.

We had one, sometimes two, cows which we milked twice a day. Mom always had a churn full of milk sitting near the fireplace.

Rotating it often kept it evenly warm. When it became softly solid, it was time to churn. She would then sit there moving the dasher up and down through a wooden lid, which had a hole in the center for the handle of the dasher, until the butter was formed on top. She would skim off the butter, rinse it, and beat it until all the water was gone, put it in a dish and place it on the shelf—no refrigeration. She poured the milk into pitchers or jars. We drank buttermilk at least twice a day. No one ever drank "sweet" milk. That was only for coffee, or to pour over blackberry or mulberry cobbler.

Breakfast was usually hot biscuits, eggs, and gravy. Then donning our school clothes, which we were not allowed to wear any other time, we would start the almost two-mile walk to school. Other children joined us along the way. There were always games and chatter, and soon the schoolhouse would be in sight.

Lunches were never provided at school. We carried our little metal lard buckets, packed with green beans and cornbread and perhaps a tomato or cucumber. In winter it was pinto beans or simply buttermilk with cornbread crumbled into it. I loved it when the milk got a bit icy by lunch time.

The walk was not so pleasant when it was raining or snowing. I can remember reaching home many times with ice on the legs of my trousers. Mom always made us wear trousers in winter, though no one else wore them. There were several places where we had to cross a creek. It was fun jumping from one rock to another avoiding getting our feet wet. But when the creeks flooded, it was terrifying. There were times when we couldn't follow the road at all, but had to go around the mountainside to avoid having to cross the water. My oldest sister Ivy always took charge and got us home safely.

In the summers, Ivy often took us exploring. We roamed the farm looking for anything interesting. Sometimes we went all the way to the top of the mountain and often found huckleberries. Since there were never enough berries to pick and save for a pie, we ate them on the spot. There were huge cliffs near the top of the mountain. We would climb up the side of the huge rocks then crawl across the top. Lying on our stomachs, we would inch along until we could look over the edge. It was fun but scary, and I often had nightmares afterward.

On rainy days we often sat in the porch swing and sang—at the top of our voices! There were no neighbors near enough to hear, so we could be as loud as Mom would allow. Mom and Dad were good singers, so all of us inherited their ability to carry a tune and harmonize. It was great fun.

Daddy worked at farming the first few years of my life and worked very hard. Sometimes he worked for other farmers to have some cash for the things we couldn't provide for ourselves. He tried various other things, also. Once he started a small store. In order to bring in the supplies, he ordered a wagon from a catalog. It was painted green and red—no one else in the area ever owned a painted wagon, and we were so proud to ride in it. However, the store didn't last very long—too many people bought things on credit and didn't pay. Daddy soon realized he was losing money, so he closed it.

Raising chickens was another venture. He ordered what seemed like hundreds of small chicks. They arrived by mail, several chirping cardboard boxes of them. The boxes had small breathing holes here and there and a little contraption of water. Still, not all of the chicks survived the trip. There was also a tent and a kerosene heater. Dad set it all up, and all went well until one night when we had a big rain storm. Soon all of us were out there trying to keep the chicks warm, dry, and to keep them from suffocating each other by piling up near the heater. The chicks all made it through the storm and eventually grew and started laying eggs, hundreds of them. We gathered eggs several times a day. Mom packed them in crates, and Dad took them to market.

❖ ❖ ❖

It was a very special day when Daddy brought home our first radio. Since electricity had not yet arrived, the radio had a very big, very heavy battery with it. Daddy put both the radio and the battery up on a really high shelf so that only he and Mom could operate it. We listened to the *Lone Ranger, Our Miss Brooks,* and, of course, the news. Mom and Dad both liked country music. Mom's favorite singer was Bill Monroe. We listened to the Grand Ole Opry every Saturday night.

Daddy even tried learning radio repair several years later. He ordered the course and studied in the evenings. However, not enough people owned radios to make his knowledge profitable.

We washed laundry by rubbing the clothes on a washboard and wringing them by hand. The white things were boiled in a big wash tub or round-bottomed iron pot. A product called "bluing" was added to the rinse water to make the clothes look whiter. We hung everything outside on lines to dry, no matter how hot or cold the weather. Sometimes in winter the clothes would freeze stiff but eventually would dry. When some things needed to be dry sooner, we brought them in and hung them around the fireplace on the backs of chairs and broom handles. One night some hot coals rolled out onto the hearth too close to the clothes. A fire started and was climbing up the wall by the time Daddy awoke. He grabbed buckets of water from the kitchen and soon had it out. Smoke came up the stairs and into my bedroom. I only partially woke up, just enough to raise my window. I went back to sleep and only learned about the fire the next morning!

I loved the farm, and those first years of life are a wonderful memory. One spring day when I was about twelve, I climbed the hill alone, probably looking for hazelnuts or berries. As I crested the steep slope leading to the first plateau, I caught my breath at the beauty before me. There, to the left of the trail, where corn had been planted the previous year, was the largest field of daisies I had ever seen. It was magnificent, with the sun making each white and yellow flower glow as if trying to outshine the ones next to it. I stood there for a long time just drinking in the display of brilliance, mesmerized by the soft breeze gently swaying the flowers. I have never forgotten that scene. Throughout my life, it has always been a place I could go in my mind when the world around me was not so pleasant.

❖ ❖ ❖

While Daddy was definitely a hard worker and a good provider, he was not a very good husband. He was never faithful to my mother even at Hollybush. And when he went away from home for long periods of time, his womanizing was even worse. He fathered a child before he and Mom were married, Stellie Slone. Mom always loved her. She stayed with us often, and sometimes worked for us when Mom was not well. As she grew up and became an adult, she and Mom became very close friends. Her children called Mom "Mamaw Madge" and two of the daughters stayed with Mom for some of their high school years. Tragically, Stellie died in her fifties. After Mom died many years later, Stellie's children developed a closer relationship with Dad and visited him often.

2

Camp Nathanael

"See how great a love the Father has bestowed on us, that we would be called children of God; and such we are. For this reason the world does not know us, because it did not know Him."

1 JOHN 3:1

In 1942, for seventh grade, I went to a boarding school, located on Caney Creek just past my grandparents' home. My older sisters Ivallean and Arlene were already attending school at the Caney Community Center Schools, Ivallean in high school and Arlene in eighth grade. The schools required everyone to wear white cotton uniforms with ties, black for grade school and high school and red for college. The lady who made my uniforms said they were the smallest she had ever made. I was allowed to go home every weekend, and at least one sister went with me.

My sisters had already established a tradition which we continued for all our years at Caney. After crossing the mountain between Caney and Hollybush, we walked past the grade school and up Hollybush branch where we finally reached a very large tree on the lower side of the road. There we put down our suitcases, cupped our hands by our mouths, and called loudly, "woooweeee." Any children still at home would come running to meet us with the dog bounding along behind them, barking all the way. Everyone would talk at once, and anyone strong enough would pick up a suitcase and carry it the rest of the way home. Mom would have supper ready, and though the weekend was busy, it was always good to be home.

I finished the seventh grade at Caney and went home for the summer, just after my sister Priscilla was born. She was a beautiful, blue-eyed little girl with blonde curly hair. While Mom was recovering I became her helper, doing most of the cooking. Since Ivy and Arlene were away at summer school, there was no one else to help. I carried things to Mom's bedroom, and she would tell me how much baking powder, salt, or shortening was needed to put in the biscuits, cornbread, or whatever I was cooking. I liked cooking, and I didn't mind doing it.

Mom had regained her strength by the end of summer, so I went back to Caney with my sisters, but I wasn't happy being away from home. After a few weeks into the eighth grade year, I returned home with Mom's blessing. I was still needed at home.

Mom was so appreciative of my help that for my birthday in September she had a new dress made for me—blue and shiny. I thought it was the prettiest dress I had ever seen. When the Hollybush school put on a play that Christmas—a portion of *Les Miserables,* I was asked to play Cozette. It required that I wear rags in the beginning and be dressed up at the end. So I wore a ragged dress on top of my pretty blue one and took it off at the end. I was so proud!

Christine was already busy learning the Bible verses when I returned to the Hollybush School. Two lady Bible teachers, missionaries with the Scripture Memory Mountain Mission, had already visited the school. I started studying right away. This was no doubt God's reason for bringing me home again. By the time the ladies returned, both of us had mastered the twenty-five verses from John and were ready for our New Testaments. The ladies were delighted. We told them of our disappointment two years earlier when Mr. Hull didn't return. They assured us they would keep coming as long as we were learning the verses. We had no idea how difficult keeping that promise would be for them.

One of the ladies, Alta Mae Miller, had sparkling brown eyes, dark curly hair, and was very pretty. She always told the Bible story. The other, Joyce Garrett, was a big lady. Her hair was lighter, and she wore glasses. She had the most beautiful smile, showing perfect, gleaming teeth. Her whole face lit up when she smiled, and she was always smiling. She brought a small puppet, some kind of animal with a long tail that she carried on her left arm. Using her right hand she made the animal move and seem lifelike. She teased the students by moving the puppet up close and making it say "Hello," and she tried to get us to say "Hello" or feel his tail. Then she led the singing while playing an accordion and always coaxed us into singing with all our might. It was wonderful. We loved them both and loved having them come.

Miss Miller often used pictures with the Bible stories. Sometimes it was a large book with pictures, and sometimes she used flannelgraph. She set up an easel with a board covered in flannel. Sometimes she draped a background flannel over that before adding pictures of people and animals or sometimes trees or buildings as she told the Bible story. Such beautiful pictures. I was always mesmerized!

One story was very special. It was about a hen and her little chickens. (We were well-acquainted with chickens.) I can still see the picture of the little chicks cuddling up under the wings of the mother. Miss Miller then told us something about Jesus crying and wanting people to come to Him. "Jerusalem, Jerusalem . . . how often I wanted to gather your children together, the way a hen gathers her chicks under her wings, and you were unwilling" (Matt. 23:37). I didn't really understand it then, but I was beginning to be aware that Jesus loved me.

My recollection of that first year is hazy, but apparently the ladies could not get their car up the rough roads in the winter, and Miss Miller came alone on horseback. It was a long, cold ride on muddy roads across and through creek beds, and sometimes through rain and snow. But she came, and Christine and I kept memorizing the verses. Many years later I wrote to Joyce Garrett asking her to give me more details about those early years. The following is part of her reply:

> When I arrived [in Kentucky] in October of 1942, the Perry County schools were without workers, and Alta and I started our ministry in them, also taking some other county schools. But that was the last year that SMMM (Scripture Memory Mountain Mission) was allowed into the city school system in Perry County. That left us with more free time than we wanted—and Mr. Hull needed to be relieved of some of his jobs for more attention to the work at the campground.
>
> He took us on our first trip to the Knott Co. Schools, in his Model A Ford—all the way over to the middle Hollybush school, through Caney and down the creek to the Maryland Slone school, and Raven, and out to Beaver Creek. After he had gone the full distance that day, he said, "You will not be able to make this trip in your 1940 Chevrolet!" We were amazed that he would say such a

thing after we had presented the memory plan in all those schools and promised them that we would be back in two weeks to bring them a Bible lesson and listen to the verses. We objected, but to no avail. He just proceeded to tell us that Miss Miller could rent a horse for the day and go to all those schools. She had never ridden before. But she could learn. So she did. A few weeks later, she rented a horse and spent the day visiting all those schools by horseback! At the same time I visited alone the schools on Beaver—7 of them—and then waited at Leburn for her return. I finished my trip around 4:00. She usually arrived exhausted around 6 or 6:30.

I quote from a letter from Alta now, "How well I remember that first trip—34 miles round trip! Christine said her verses the first time. When I made the next trip, Lorrie was with her. I said, 'Who is this girl?' Christine said, 'She's my sister, Lorrie. She went to the Caney school, but she came back here so she could say the verses.'"

We eventually recited all 250 Bible verses and were eligible for camp.

When Misses Miller and Garrett came for the last visit that year, it was warm weather, and they were able to come together in their car. They promised to write us telling us the camp dates and what we needed to bring. They also said they would visit us sometime during the summer. We were both scared and excited. We had done it, and we were going to camp!

When the letter came, Mom did her best to provide all the needed items. She ordered new clothes for Christine and me from the Montgomery Ward catalog. Many of our neighbors tried to dissuade her from letting us go, saying that this religion was not what their parents had taught them, that children couldn't be saved and shouldn't go to Sunday school. Praise God, she paid no heed to them.

Miss Garrett and Miss Miller did visit our home, driving as far as they could and walking the rest of the way. Mom cooked a big meal for them, and we all enjoyed the visit.

❖ ❖ ❖

When the day to go to Camp arrived, Christine and I started on our journey early. We were to meet Miss Miller and Miss Garrett at the Caney School. It was almost two miles to the Hollybush School. Beyond that, we had a mountain to cross, and of course, we were carrying our suitcases. I had traveled the same route every weekend while attending the Caney School. The distance was shorter over the mountain when on foot. However, when Miss Miller traveled by horseback, she went around the mountain. We planned to stop and rest at our grandparents' home before going the last mile. But while we were still descending the mountain, it started to rain. We hurried and made it before getting too wet, but my carefully curled hair was now straight. Christine's was naturally curly, so it just curled up tighter.

We waited in vain for the rain to stop. For a long time it just poured down. Finally it let up a little, and we started on with only our sweaters over our heads. As we neared the school we saw them. Miss Miller was already outside the car wearing a raincoat and boots, ready to start walking to meet us. It was still raining some, and we were wet to the skin but happy to be on our way, and the car was warm.

They took us to their home for the night. Though modest by many standards and smaller than our house, it was the prettiest house I had ever seen. The curtains were white and frilly, and everything was so colorful and sparklingly *clean*! It seemed like a dream. Then it was supper time. We were both very shy, which added to our discomfort.

We struggled to cut the meat for a while, trying to copy our hostesses. Finally, Christine's went flying off her plate. Miss Garrett then kindly offered to cut the meat for both of us, and we gratefully accepted.

When it was time for bed, we were asked where our pajamas were. We had never slept in pajamas and didn't have any. We always slept in our slips. I lied, saying we forgot them, but I'm sure they knew the truth. We slept without any that night, but the next day Miss Miller found some for us, probably at the children's home located on the Camp Nathanael property. We had never seen a real bath tub either. We always bathed in a wash tub, so the bath was a great delight. The next day the ladies drove us over to camp.

After traveling about twenty minutes, we turned off the highway, crossed a bridge, and turned onto a tree-lined, dirt road so narrow that the branches of the treetops intertwined. With the sun streaming through the multi-shaded green leaves, it looked like a magical tunnel and was definitely taking us to a place which would impact the rest of our lives.

After about a quarter of a mile, the road opened up to a large, green, beautiful valley. The first building we saw was the small stone chapel, which looked really huge to me then. Built of large, blue-gray stones, it had an impressive outside stairway leading up to the chapel and offices. The kitchen and dining room were on the ground floor. Directly across from the chapel was a large, white building called The Homestead. It housed a number of orphan children. Between these two buildings was a wide, grassy meadow.

At the far end of the meadow, stood two barracks-type buildings. Chris and I were taken to the first one, our home for the week. The building had screen on the upper half of the two long sides and galvanized panels on the two ends. The floors were sawdust. All the girl campers lived in this building. The boys lived in a similar building further down the valley.

Everyone slept on folding cots and bathed in wash basins. Food was served on tin plates, which we helped wash. At the opposite end of the meadow, past the Homestead and to the left, was the outdoor chapel with benches made of logs. Down the embankment was the swimming hole, a part of Troublesome Creek. (A few years later the camp installed a swimming pool down close to where the "dorms" had been.) It was all absolutely wonderful. Though we were timid, we couldn't resist the joyful atmosphere and joined in heartily in all the singing and activities.

How we loved the daily visits to the outdoor chapel when Miss Garrett led all the campers in singing and taught us many songs. She always explained the meaning of the songs and talked about how wonderful the Lord was. She seemed so happy and made singing such fun. There were also games, swimming, hikes in the woods, and delicious food.

But the Bible classes and the nightly chapel services brought about the biggest changes in my life. The devotional times in our cabin before going to bed also made a great impression. I heard my first foreign missionary that week, a lady from China. She taught us to sing "Jesus Loves Me" in Chinese. I still remember most of it. Her stories of the Chinese people really touched my heart.

What a great treat it was when a lady named Miss Margaret Slaughter, whom everyone called Aunt Peg, would tell a story. She was the best storyteller I have ever heard even to this day. There could be a hundred children in the room while she was talking, and you could hear a pin drop! All eyes were fastened on her. I learned many great truths while spellbound by her stories.

On the way to their home, Miss Miller asked us if either of us had ever asked Jesus to come into our heart and save us. Christine said "no," but I answered "yes." During my stay at Caney, Reverend J. S. Bell from Hindman Baptist Church visited the school each week conducting a chapel service. Also, once a year he held a week of revival services. I realized I was a sinner and needed to let God change my heart during some of those meetings. I wanted to be saved, but I'm not sure when my salvation took place. I'm just thankful God did forgive my sins and make me His child.

Christine went forward in one of the evening meetings at Camp Nathanael. Only the fact that I told Miss Miller I was already saved kept me from going with her. After the week was over, we determined to read our Bibles every night before going to sleep, and we did for a while. But we soon became negligent. Mom told us later that she was disappointed when she realized we had stopped, but she didn't say anything at the time.

❖ ❖ ❖

When I finished the eighth grade, I returned to Caney for high school. I was 11 years old. I could barely carry the books we had to take to the dorm every night and carry to classes the next day. Sometimes older, stronger girls would help me. Some just teased. I always felt so much less than others. While others seemed so grown up, and the girls seemed so beautiful, I was just a young short kid.

The next two years I made little spiritual progress. I went to camp both summers, and each time I sincerely rededicated my life to God, but each time after a few weeks or months, I returned to my old ways. If there had been a church and Sunday school to attend, things might have been different. As it was, our one week of camp in the summer and Rev. Bell's chapel services were all the instruction we received, and there were many adverse pressures.

A church in Hollybush met once a month in the summer, but our family seldom attended. They were very strict in some ways. They felt it was a terrible sin to cut your hair or wear makeup or jewelry. Salvation was based on a vision or dream. They were wonderful sincere people, who I'm sure loved God, but they didn't know the Scriptures very well. Rev. J. S. Bell was not highly regarded because he held Sunday school in his church and baptized people indoors, which they believed was wrong.

Grandma Caudill always talked about being baptized in the winter. The ice had to be broken for her to be baptized in the creek, but she didn't get a cold—a sign to her that she was truly righteous. They didn't believe that children could be saved. One preacher once said to me, "When you get a little older, you'll learn better." Praise God I did learn that they were wrong. Children can be saved at any age.

I did continue memorizing Bible verses. I met the ladies at the Caney school on their way back from Hollybush, where Christine was still faithful with her memorizing. Later I said the verses to others who reported to Misses Miller and Garrett. The second year we memorized the same 250 verses as the first year, thus solidifying them in our minds. The third year we memorized the book of 1 John. After that we were "free campers."

It would be impossible to relate how much memorizing those verses has meant to me over the years. I really discovered why it is so important to hide God's Word in our hearts (Ps.119:11). So many times when I was troubled, afraid, or in any kind of need, one of the verses would pop into my mind, and the Lord always met my need through His Word.

❖ ❖ ❖

In early 1944, Daddy received a letter from the US Government. Though he had six children, he had to answer the draft and joined the US Army that April. In the induction process, he had to fill out several forms and provide his marriage license. But when he checked with the county court house, he found that the marriage had never been recorded. Fortunately, the man who performed the ceremony was still alive. He signed the necessary papers and got it recorded. Mom and Dad thought it would have been funny had they needed to have the ceremony over again, taking all six children to the "wedding."

Daddy never went overseas but spent most of his time in Arkansas guarding German prisoners. We children didn't understand much about the war, just that Daddy was gone. Mom cried when his clothes were sent back to her (the usual practice at the time), saying it was like he had died. He came home for a visit once or twice, and Mom went to visit him once, staying about a week. She came back telling us about the "funny" way people talked in that state. She also came back pregnant, her ninth pregnancy. Daddy came home in December of 1945.

3

A New Town

> "The Lord is compassionate and gracious, slow to anger
> and abounding in lovingkindness."
>
> PSALM 103:8

In March of 1946, Arlene and I were at Caney when we heard the baby Mom had carried was stillborn, and Mom was very ill. We went home to attend the funeral. Neighbors came and built a small wooden box for a coffin. Our little sister, who was named Donna Phyllis, was buried beside the other two babies who had died years earlier. I remember Mom crying and not being able to attend the funeral. The baby had apparently died *in utero* about the eighth month. By the time she was born, Mom was near death herself. She was sick for months. She developed phlebitis, vein inflammation, in one leg, and though it healed, she had trouble with that leg for the rest of her life.

Fortunately, Daddy was out of the Army and at home. To his credit, Daddy was devoted to Mom during her long months of illness. He spent hours reading to her, bathing her, bringing her food, and feeding her when necessary. A doctor came from the nearest town to help, and Mom eventually recovered. I believe Daddy did always love my mother. He just had a problem being attracted to other women.

New Kids in Town

Later that year, just after I started my junior year of high school at Caney, Arlene and I heard that our parents had moved to a small coal mining town where our father had started working in the mines. Ivallean attended Berea College for nurse's training, and Christine had not yet started high school, so it was just Arlene and me at Caney. Mom needed to have easier access to a doctor, so Daddy found a house near his work, rented a truck, and moved them. They weren't able to contact us directly but wanted us to remain at Caney. We had no such idea! This new town sounded to us like an exciting place to go to school. So we made plans to join them right away.

We must have borrowed the money for the bus fare. We never had that much cash on hand. We had no "civilian" clothes so we wore our uniforms. Others told us how to go and somehow, perhaps by a letter, we learned approximately where our family lived. We set out on a Friday afternoon. Arlene and I rode with another student and her parents to a place where there was a "Y" in the road. There we waited for the bus.

Neither of us had ever ridden a bus, but we were instructed to wait for the one that had the town's name written on the front. It was a long time in coming, so we walked along the highway for quite a distance. We debated whether the bus would stop for us upon seeing our suitcases, or if we should flag it. I certainly didn't have the nerve to flag it, but Arlene decided rather than to risk missing it, she would. At last we saw the bus coming, and Arlene stuck out her arm. The bus stopped, and we climbed aboard and went immediately to a seat about midway back. All the passengers looked at us curiously, and the driver called back asking where we were going. We thought that was a silly question since the bus had the name written on the front. Nevertheless, we answered him with the name of the town. Along the way, as other passengers got on, paid their fares, and others got off at various places, we figured things out a bit and began to feel quite embarrassed that we had not paid when we boarded.

At the end of the line, we were the last to get off. We apologized, paid our fare, and asked for directions. "Just go straight ahead," the bus driver said, "until you come to the end of the highway. The road branches off there."

Friends told us later that they thought we were either a strange sort of nurses or nuns. Little realizing the spectacle we made in our white uniforms, including white stockings and shoes, we started the last lap of our journey on foot. It was farther than we expected, and our suitcases seemed to grow heavier all the time. We asked a few people if they knew where our parents lived, but no one seemed to know. It was beginning to get late, and we were starting to get worried

Finally we found a young girl who went to school with Christine. We had passed the house. Following her instructions we finally found the house just as it was getting dark. Mom and Dad were surprised to see us, but they didn't make us return to Caney.

The house they lived in was very small, only three rooms and a very small kitchen. It was almost like being back in the one-room place. Going to school in "the big city" was not what we expected either. There were lots of complications. For instance, we had very few "normal" clothes, and there was no money to buy any. So we had to wear the same ones over and over.

We were soon caught up in the wanting-to-be-like-everyone-else disease. Though I was only thirteen and as always, looked even younger, most of my classmates were sixteen, seventeen, or older. They all wore makeup, so I wore makeup, too. I must have looked ridiculous. Mom didn't forbid me to wear it, but she tried to persuade me that I was not old enough. Finally I did learn to apply it more lightly.

At Caney, boys and girls were kept very separate. They were never allowed to sit on the same side of the room. Dating also was not allowed, and there were no dances or movies to attend. But in this town things were very different. There were lots of dances and parties with kissing games, though most of the boys kissed me on the cheek. There were movies when there was money for them, which was not very often. I started dating, though most of my classmates considered me a "kid." I shudder to think of those years, but praise God for His protection in spite of my worldliness and ignorance. I even tried smoking once since many of my friends smoked. But I was well aware that I could never afford to buy the cigarettes, so I refused any offered to me after that first one. There are some advantages to being poor!

When summer came, Miss Miller and Miss Garrett came to take Christine and me to camp. I was ashamed to go, knowing I had not been living like a Christian should. But the memory of the happy times at camp drew me, and I consented to go. At camp, I resisted the Lord for a long time, not wanting to repeat the experiences of past years. But before camp was over, I had once again given my life to God. The counselors were all so kind and loving and happy. I longed to be like them. As we traveled home, I boldly wore the bright red "N" with one white stripe, which stood for my four summers at Camp Nathanael, pinned to my dress. The red stood for the blood of Jesus and the white for a cleansed heart. I was determined to witness to anyone who noticed it. But how weak I was! And how little I knew about the "wiles of the devil."

Christine and I were walking the distance from the bus station to our home when a former boyfriend overtook us.

"Where've you been?" he asked.

"To camp," I answered.

"Oh, what kind of camp?"

"It's a Christian camp," I answered feebly. He smiled. Then with a little smirk he asked, "And what were *you* doing at a Christian camp?" I did manage to say, "I'm a Christian." But that was as far as I got. The conversation abruptly changed, and I had not been nearly as bold as I had hoped.

That last year in high school, some of my classmates did realize I was a Christian, but my testimony was very weak. God is so patient with us. So were Miss Miller and Miss Garrett. They never quit trying and never gave up hope, though I'm sure that at times, hope was very low. And they never stopped praying. How I praise God for them both.

Again, the next summer, they came to take Christine and me to camp. I'm sure I was responsible for dragging Christine down many times, but she was always ready to go even though I wasn't. My clothes were clean and ironed but not packed. I didn't want to go and told Miss Garrett that I wasn't a Christian. "Oh yes you are!" she said and would not leave without me. My mother joined in the pleading, and eventually I gave in. I marvel now that my clothes were always at least partially ready, and I was always persuaded to go—no doubt in answer to the many prayers of Miss Miller and Miss Garrett and others. Mom always wanted us to go to camp also. I did greatly long to be a dedicated Christian who served the Lord, but I was easily swayed in the opposite direction. I would hear of others who were good witnesses in their homes and some who brought others to the Lord, and my heart would ache, but little change would take place.

❖ ❖ ❖

In 1949, I graduated from high school and planned to return to Caney for the two years of college they offered. (It is now a four-year school called Alice Lloyd College.) Before the school year began, my parents moved back to Hollybush. I was really glad. I had never been happy in that town, never really fit in. The houses we rented were small and dilapidated, nothing like the ten-room farm house in Hollybush. I think I longed to be back in a place where life was simpler, with fewer things to entice me in the wrong direction. At any rate, the whole family rejoiced when we returned to our old home.

During my last year of high school, Daddy was hurt in the mines, with damage to his back and one leg. After months of suffering with terrible pain and not able to work, he had surgery on his back. The ambulance brought him all the way up to our house in Hollybush following the surgery. While the attendants carried him into the house, his father arrived, red-faced and breathing hard from walking fast. "Is he dead?" he asked, looking very distraught. He and Grandma saw the ambulance pass their house, and thinking it was a hearse, feared the worst. Mom quickly assured him that Daddy was okay and took him inside to see for himself.

When Daddy recovered from the surgery, he started looking for different work. After several months of unemployment, he decided to go to Michigan and began working for the Chrysler Corporation. He came home very infrequently.

In the fall, I returned to Caney College along with Arlene, who had finished her first year of college. Christine went with us, attending Caney High School. Ivallean had finished her nurse's training at Berea College and was at The Frontier Nursing Service in Hyden, Kentucky, training in Midwifery. Chad and Priscilla were still in grade school at Hollybush.

4

No Turning Back

"Fall down seven times, get up eight."

AN OLD CHINESE PROVERB

"Bless the Lord, O my soul, and forget none of His benefits: who pardons all your iniquities."

PSALM 103:2, 3A

My sister Arlene was beginning her second year of college at Caney, and we were assigned a room together. It was not a happy arrangement, because she and I did not have the close relationship that Christine and I always enjoyed. Arlene was prone to quarrelling, and I had a quick temper. There were a number of verbal explosions. We were both taking teaching courses. Several students from our former school were enrolled at Caney College. Even our old homeroom teacher had transferred and was now one of the main instructors in the teaching courses.

A crisis came early in the year. In one of my classes, the former homeroom teacher got on the subject of how children admire and copy their teachers. "You have to watch what you do and say when you are in the classroom," she said, "for you are apt to see or hear one of your pupils doing or saying the same thing a bit later." Everyone smiled, and there followed several amusing examples of children copying their teachers—walking the same way, combing their hair the same way, etc. This little incident, likely insignificant to most of the class, became life-changing for me. It was what God used to bring me back to Himself, never to return to the world.

I couldn't help thinking that if children really copied their teachers, then I needed to be a very committed Christian. It would certainly grieve me if I should ever be the cause of some little one drifting into sin. On the other hand, what a joy it would be to be able to lead them in the right direction. I could not get it out of my thinking. I played it over and over in my mind, especially when I went to bed at night. Finally, I yielded to the Holy Spirit. I knelt beside my bed and prayed, "Lord, I don't even know if I'm saved or not, I've been so far away from You. If I'm not, save me now. Never let me doubt it again and never let me turn away from serving You. I give myself totally to You."

What a loving, longsuffering, forgiving, and wonderful heavenly Father! He answered quickly and gave me assurance that He had heard me and saved me. From that moment on I was His, and I never doubted it again. I was fifteen. It had been more than seven years since the Bible teacher, Mr. Hull, came to my school.

That was the beginning of my life long training by God, the Master Teacher. I knew at once that I must be diligent in my Bible reading and prayer and let nothing keep me from it or make me be ashamed of it. Each night I began reading a little while before the lights went out and praying after they were out. Arlene noticed of course, and it was not long before I saw that she too had started reading her Bible. One night she told me that she had asked Jesus to come into her life and to save her. What a joy! My first reward for totally surrendering my life to Christ. Things were different in that room now. We still had our old natures of quarrelling and hot temper, but we now had God's power with us. He could help us overcome the problems.

Of course I wrote to Miss Miller and Miss Garrett. They were very happy, though knowing of my many failings, perhaps were somewhat skeptical. They never let me know of any doubts, however. They were always encouraging, and most of all, they never ceased to pray and to demonstrate their love.

I found out later about another intercessor. Christine and I had been able to go to Camp Nathanael for free. That is, having learned the Scripture verses, we were not asked to pay any money for the weeks at camp. But since the camp had to have some means of supplying the food and other necessities, each Christian worker was asked to find a sponsor for each child he or she brought to camp. A lady in Michigan, Mrs. Ione Smith, a friend of Joyce Garrett's, became the sponsor for Christine and me. She sent in the first twenty dollars needed for Christine and me that first year, and probably many succeeding years. She also added us to her daily prayer list, and we were never taken off. From that day until her death some fifteen years later that dear lady brought us before the throne of grace daily. I was on the mission field when I heard of her death. I'm sure her prayers were partly responsible for my being there.

I attempted witnessing again and found that my witnessing didn't fall flat as before. I had some good conversations with several girls. I also discovered that there were a few Christians in our dorm, and I greatly enjoyed their friendship. I didn't know many hymns since we had sung mostly choruses at Camp Nathanael. One girl spent many hours teaching me some of the most-loved hymns.

When we were at home, Arlene, Christine, and I started a family devotional time. We would gather the family together, choose a portion of Scripture, and take turns reading a verse each. Then those of us who were saved would pray. When Ivallean was home, she would also join in the praying for she had accepted Jesus as her Savior during a conference she attended at Camp Nathanael. One night, after the three of us prayed, Mom started praying. She thanked God for saving her, for a few other things, and said "Amen." We were startled but overjoyed, and I think most of us were laughing and crying at the same time. She told us she thought she had been a Christian for many years but lacked assurance. She also shared with us that before she was married she was dating two young men. One day she went out in the garden and prayed asking God which one she should marry. She felt that God told her to marry Daddy. That had helped her to believe that God was real and that He answered prayer.

Starting the reading and praying with the family had been difficult—it is not easy for children to lead the parents, but now we were abundantly rewarded. Of the whole family this left only Daddy and the youngest sister, Priscilla, who were not saved. Christine and I helped our brother, Chad, learn the Bible verses one year. While at Camp Nathanael that summer, he made a profession of faith, although he never gave much evidence of knowing the Lord his whole life. Only God knows what was in his heart. Several years later, Priscilla also learned all the Bible verses and went to Camp Nathanael along with a friend from Hollybush, and while there she asked Jesus to come into her heart. She and Mom started going to the family conferences at the camp. So Camp Nathanael meant a great deal to my whole family.

❖ ❖ ❖

After Daddy was hurt in the mines and had surgery, he was unable to work for several months. He tried in vain to get some compensation from the mining company. Our financial needs became desperate. So we prayed often about it. Daddy once again went to see the mining company officials to ask what could be done. While he was gone, we again asked God to intervene. When Daddy returned he had six hundred dollars with him! That was a lot of money in those days. In addition, he also received some monthly benefits. Though I knew Daddy was not eager to do so, I suggested we go to prayer again and thank God for bringing this blessing to pass. I don't know how it affected the rest of the family, but I know *my* faith was greatly strengthened.

Camp that summer was pure joy. It was the first time I had gone without a guilty conscience and sorely needing a change in my heart.

Back at Caney the next year, I was given the responsibility of being housemother for one of the dorms, housing about fifteen or sixteen girls. It put me in an excellent position for witnessing. There were a few other Christian girls, and together we started dorm devotions in two of the girls' dorms, with one of us usually taking charge. I was still pretty shy and found this very hard to do, so I let others handle it as often as they were willing. I had some good private talks with several of the girls. Many of them seemed interested, but alas many of them were only "almost persuaded."

One night during one of these discussions, one girl said, "You think we're more interested than we are; we're interested but . . ." Her voice trailed off. In other words, she didn't want to be pushed. Perhaps I had been pushing them too much in my eagerness. Still, putting off salvation to "some other time" is one of Satan's favorite devices. And many who put it off never make that all-important decision.

When Rev. Bell came to the school for his usual revival meetings, there was a great response. Many people went forward saying they wanted to accept Jesus as their Savior. I was comforted in thinking that at least I had a part in the "sowing" and "watering" ("I planted, Apollos watered, but God was causing the growth" 1 Cor. 3:6.) Some of the new converts did turn back to their old lives before the year was out, but perhaps they were like me, turning back many times before becoming strong in their faith. I trust many of them eventually surrendered to God.

That fall Christine and I began thinking we should be baptized and join a church. So we decided to ask Rev. Bell about it. He was quite happy, of course. We needed a time for the baptism when we would not be in school. So we set the date for Christmas Day which fell on a Sunday that year. We persuaded an uncle to take us in his truck. Because of his belief that baptisms should not be performed indoors, he would not enter the church. He waited outside for us until the service was over.

Candidates for baptism were usually asked to wear white, so we wore our uniforms, minus the ties. We were then baptized in a heated indoor baptistery! The ladies who assisted us were so nice and helpful. We had never even seen anyone baptized before. But all went well. Afterward we made the long trip back home in the back of the truck. (It did have a cover.) And it was snowing! We didn't catch a cold. I have always thought this was for my grandmother's sake. It was the Lord using her own standard for righteousness to show her that we too were accepted by God.

The uncle who took us later accepted Christ as his Savior, as did his wife, my Mom's sister, and most of their children. The whole family became very active in one of Rev. Bell's branch churches.

I was amazed at the effect being baptized had on my Christian life. I had now joined a church. I had publically declared my faith in Jesus Christ and had demonstrated my commitment to the Lord by being baptized. There was no turning back now. I was committed. The finality of it made me more settled, stronger, and aware that I belonged to God forever.

5

A Different Kind of College

"Make me know Your ways, O Lord, teach me Your paths.
Lead me in Your truth and teach me, for You are the God
of my salvation; for You I wait all the day."

PSALM 25:4, 5

As the school year of 1951 drew to a close, I naturally started wondering what I should do in the future. Caney was only a junior college. Arlene was already teaching at the Hollybush School. She had also started a Sunday school in the school building. I was not really interested in teaching, and I was still so young and immature. I was definitely not ready to enter the adult work world. Miss Garrett and Miss Miller started talking to me about going to a Bible Institute or Christian College. I *did* want to go because I realized I didn't know much about the Bible, but I had no money for that kind of schooling. The only reason I had been able to attend at Caney was that it was almost free. I am eternally grateful for the good education that school provided for me and my sisters, as well as a couple of years for my brother.

Miss Miller told me about how she and her older sister, who was at that time a missionary in Africa, had gone to a Bible College "by faith." That is, by depending on God alone to supply their needs. It was the first time I had heard that phrase. Her younger sister, Helen, was attending William Jennings Bryan University in much the same way.

On Easter weekend, Christine and I were invited to come to Hardburly where Misses Garrett and Miller lived to spend a few days with them. We were to take a bus to Bulan where the road to Hardburly branched off, and Miss Garrett would pick us up at a restaurant there. But for some reason I did not mail my answer to them soon enough, so they didn't receive my letter and assumed we weren't coming. Not knowing that anything had changed, Christine and I took the bus to Bulan and sat down in the restaurant to wait. We waited and waited and waited, but no Miss Garrett. We didn't know what to do. We couldn't go back home. There were no more buses. We found out too late that there had been a bus going to Hardburly.

I began thinking about a taxi, but I only had one dollar and was afraid that one dollar wasn't enough to pay the fare. Finally, as it started to get dark, and closing time for the restaurant was approaching, the waitress came over and asked what the trouble was. Almost at the point of tears, I told her our situation. After some time, she found a man with a truck who lived in Hardburly and was willing to take us with him for my last dollar. With great relief, but with a great deal of discomfort at having to ride with a complete stranger, we climbed into his truck. He did not take us all the way, however, only to where he lived. We had to walk the rest of the way, about half a mile. Fear seized me again as I began thinking the ladies might not be home. What would we do then? But they *were* home and greatly surprised when they answered our knock at the door. Of course they welcomed us with open arms, and the confusion about the letter was soon sorted out.

Alta Miller's sister, Helen, and her roommate, Joan, were there from Bryan University—the reason they had invited us, no doubt. Helen's adoptive father, Harold Hillegas, was also there. It was a very enjoyable weekend in every way. There was much talk of Bryan University and how God had supplied their needs. Both Helen and Joan worked at the school while doing their studies. In addition, money came in from various sources, and the school was sympathetic when bill payments were a bit late. Christine and I took all of this in and thought about it often after Joyce took us home.

On another weekend Miss Garrett and Miss Miller were planning to take Roselyn and David Franklin, children of Garland Franklin, back to Bryan and offered to take me along to see the school. It was a long drive but a great deal of fun. We did a lot of singing. Roselyn had an exceptionally beautiful voice, as did Joyce Garrett, and some were good with harmony. What a blessing it was to sing hymn after hymn as well as choruses. When we reached the school after driving up the gentle slope of Bryan Hill, I was awestruck with the beauty of the campus. Lots of trees and flowers adorned the area in front of the main building. Several benches were scattered here and there where students could sit and study or visit.

I was introduced to everyone as a "prospective student," but I wasn't so sure. I was very much afraid of everything. This was real civilization, and this was probably my first time out of Kentucky. In spite of everything, however, I really wanted to go to school there. We met Helen's boyfriend, Dick (whom she later married), and several other students who all were very nice and friendly.

We stayed the night. I stayed with Helen in her dorm room. I vividly remember trying to take a shower the next morning. I had never seen a shower. Even at Caney, we bathed in basins, and at home it was a wash tub. I was too embarrassed to ask for help, so I just kept trying things until I got a little water running over me and had a semblance of a shower. Then I dressed quickly since others were waiting for the shower. When Miss Miller and Miss Garrett joined us, we talked to some of the administration and teachers and were given a handful of literature. I accepted a catalog and an application form, just in case.

Then we had the long trip back. It was after dark when we arrived back at Caney, later than we were supposed to be out, but my explanation about our trip kept me from getting into trouble.

Miss Miller advised me to tear out the page from the Bryan catalog on which the expenses were listed, and put it in the corner of my mirror. That way, every time I looked at my mirror and saw the list, I would be reminded to pray that God would provide. I followed her suggestion and added Philippians 4:19, "And my God will supply all your needs according to His riches in glory in Christ Jesus." I also sent in my application.

When the letter came accepting my application, it then became necessary to send in a $10.00 room deposit as a confirmation of my intention to go. This brought the situation to a head. Before this time I had gone forward with uncertainty—I could still back out. But now I must decide. When the room deposit went in, I was committed. Of course, I didn't have $10.00 to send, and this brought about a testing of my faith. So I prayed, "Lord, I must know Your will. If it is Your will that I go trusting You to supply, then provide this first $10.00 as a token and a sign to me that You will provide all that is needed." Then I added, "And please send it in such a way that I'll know it's from You."

Graduation was drawing near. Each year at Commencement, every graduating high-school and college student was required to give an extemporaneous speech, and prizes were given. The high school boy and girl who gave the best speeches won five dollars each. The winners of the best college speeches were given $10.00 each. I didn't even *think* of connecting this with my prayer, for in all the years at Caney neither I nor either of my sisters had ever won a prize. We didn't have the confidence to make good speeches.

But this time, when I walked up on the platform and received my little slip of paper, I saw that one word was written on it—Christianity. I was pleased, for this was a subject I was passionate about. I simply gave my testimony, saying something at the beginning about Christianity being about a person—Jesus Christ. At the end I said, "I wish each of you here tonight knew Jesus Christ as I know Him."

I returned to my seat still having no thought of winning. Whoever heard of winning a speech contest by giving a testimony. But when the prizes were given out, I was handed an envelope containing ten beautiful dollars! I had no doubt that it came from God, and I mailed the room deposit the very next day.

A few weeks later, it was necessary for me to go to the town of Hazard, about fifteen miles from my home, to complete the physical exam required by Bryan University. As I always did whenever possible, I stopped on my way for a visit with my grandparents on Caney Creek. My grandmother had been very sick for several months and was much worse that morning. Still, she recognized me. I was her namesake, and she always told me I was her favorite. She asked my aunts, who were there caring for her, to help her up to a chair. She tried to talk, but was very weak. After a while, I said good-bye to them all and went on my way.

When I returned in the afternoon, an acquaintance met me before I reached my grandparents' home and told me my grandmother was dead and that she had already been taken to the funeral home. What a shock! In the morning she was on earth, and in the afternoon she was in heaven. Other than my stillborn sister, Donna Phyllis, it was my first experience with death so close in the family. How glad I was that she knew the Lord. And how wonderful it was to have the Comforter with me in times of grief.

❖ ❖ ❖

Miss Miller and Miss Garrett entered wholeheartedly into what they called, "getting our daughter ready to go off to college." They made clothes for me, even a lovely lavender evening gown. They embroidered my initials on sheets and pillowcases, and they stirred up others to help also. What they provided for me was far more than what my parents could provide. At last the day came to leave for Bryan College. Christine went with us. Helen and her father, who came down from Wisconsin, were also along. In a separate car, a friend I had met at camp, Lajena Barker, was going as a freshman. Her parents accompanied her. The trip was all the more joyous with so many friends with us.

When we arrived on Bryan Hill, Miss Miller and Miss Garrett took me into the office and paid one hundred dollars on my room and board. I didn't know then what a sacrifice they were making to pay the expenses of the trip, for all the clothes and other items, and to give that amount of money. How I praise God for them! And for all the Christian workers who willingly give their all to see young people brought to the Lord and trained for His service.

Lajena and I were close friends during both my years at Bryan. It was a great comfort for me to have such a close friend. I hated to go anywhere alone. She was much more outgoing than I and helped me make other friends. But there were many problems. The studies were very difficult. I had always done well academically, but this was unfamiliar territory. Entering Bryan as a junior put me in junior and senior classes. Others in those classes had already completed Old and New Testament Survey, and a good number of other biblical subjects.

I was just beginning to learn the Bible, and even most of the freshmen knew more than I did. Only occasionally would I discover someone who was perhaps newly saved, or transferred from a secular college who was struggling as I was.

One class was particularly distressing—philosophy. Imagine my dismay when the discussions were on such terms as "neo-orthodoxy" or "liberalism." I did manage to pass all my classes, though in a class on Ephesians, just barely.

My experience with a French-language course proved God's presence with me and turned out to be a blessing. I had taken the first year of French my freshman year at Caney. I attempted to take the advanced course my first year at Bryan. But I found it so difficult and the teacher so unhelpful that I dropped out. Nevertheless, the next year I discovered the school required another year of a foreign language to graduate. I was forced to try the French course again. This time I went to the Lord in prayer. "Lord," I prayed, "I know if I can learn to like the subject and the teacher, it won't be so hard to study and learn. Please help me to like them both."

God answered my prayer, and the instructor became one of my favorite teachers. I had misunderstood his impish good humor as being callous and uncaring. A few doors down from my room in the dormitory lived the Assistant Dean of Women, who graduated the year before, majoring in French. I went to her for help. She was especially kind and patient. She spent many hours tutoring me until I felt I had caught up with the rest of the class. I ended with a good grade. The experience was a great stimulus to my faith, helping me to know how God is interested in every phase of our lives. We only have to ask for His help.

Another difficulty was my accent, poor grammar, and "hillbilly" ways, which became a constant source of ridicule and embarrassment. Sometimes I was teased mercilessly. At first I had only to be asked where I was from and answer "Kentucky" to cause an outburst of laughter. Finally I learned to put less stress on the "tuck" and to speed it up a bit. Then I could at least get past my first word before being laughed at. I was terribly aware of my lack of training in etiquette, my dowdy clothes, and my country accent. Though the school was located in Dayton, Tennessee, northern states had a larger representation in the student body than southern states.

Adding to my social struggles was the fact that during my years at Caney, I was required to walk past the male students without speaking. Some of the male students at Bryan told me later that at first they considered me "stuck up." I was probably the least "stuck up" student of the whole Bryan family. I never considered quitting, but it was a very difficult time for me. However, God helped me learn skills that were helpful to me for the rest of my life.

Financial strains continued throughout both years at Bryan. Though, praise the Lord, I graduated with only a small debt, which I was able to pay off in a few months after graduating. Considering that I arrived at school with only five dollars in my pocket, that was no small miracle. Miss Miller and Miss Garrett had continued to help as much as they could and almost always came to take me home for vacations and took me back afterward.

I worked also, usually as a waitress in the school dining room. Meals were served restaurant style, with waiters and waitresses. Seats were assigned and everything was done very properly. No one left the dining room until everyone was finished eating, and a hymn was always sung before dispersing. I loved the wonderful acoustics and beautiful harmony of those hymns. I don't think I have ever heard such beautiful singing since those years.

Many unexpected gifts helped my financial situation. Friends of Miss Miller and Miss Garrett sometimes wrote to me and sent gifts. A man visiting Bryan who had seen my picture and testimony in a

Camp Nathanael periodical, gave me a gift of money. Another time, a lady named Mrs. Cousins sent me a beautiful yellow blouse, a black skirt, and a hat for Easter. So the Lord provided as He had promised. Miss Garrett and Miss Miller taught me to rely on Phillippians 4:6: "Be anxious for nothing, but in everything by prayer and supplication with thanksgiving let your requests be made known to God." And Philippians 4:19, "And my God shall supply all your needs." God was true to His Word. He was big enough to meet every need.

During all those difficulties, the Lord was always my helper. Those I worked with became my friends, and I slowly began feeling more comfortable with everything. I was also slowly growing spiritually. Through the Bible courses and Chapel services, I was getting to know the Bible better. I attended church regularly and had some good examples of godly young people in my roommates and friends, as well as in the teachers and staff.

My second year was less stressful. I made more friends, learned a few more social skills, and made better grades. I am very grateful for my two years at Bryan.

❖ ❖ ❖

Near the end of my second year, Helen surprised us all by announcing, "My sister is marrying my father!" It was true! When their parents died, Helen and her younger brother were adopted by Mr. and Mrs. Hillegas. Alta Miller and her older sister were in college, and didn't need to be adopted. Later, Mrs. Hillegas died. Through the years of visiting back and forth, Mr. Hillegas and Alta became very good friends, and eventually decided to marry, making Alta Helen's step-mother as well as her sister. Alta then moved to Wisconsin, and Joyce Garrett was left without a co-worker. Perhaps she thought of my helping her from the beginning, but the thought didn't occur to me until later.

In the meantime, I had a boyfriend. It started while I was home for Christmas when I agreed to a blind date arranged by a relative. After returning to school, I received a letter from the blind date requesting that I correspond with him. He was not a believer, and I hesitated but decided to write to him—once. I told him I was a Christian, attending a Christian school and that my letters would naturally be about God and the activities of the school. If that was what he wanted to hear, I was willing to write.

To my surprise, he answered saying that was exactly what he wanted to hear because of a promise he had made to God a few years earlier. My next letter then urged him to make a decision soon. Salvation is not to be put off, and he must keep his promise. I suggested that he talk to Rev. Bell. When I opened his next letter I found him praising the Lord for his salvation!

We continued writing, and we dated when I came home after graduation. Eventually we became engaged. I think the relationship was based on gratefulness on his part and a nurturing feeling on my part. It was not in God's plan, but we misunderstood it for a while. When the subject arose about my going to work with Miss Garrett, he was not in favor, though he didn't openly oppose it.

I worked at Camp Nathanael that summer as a counselor and enjoyed great blessing in seeing some of my girls come to know the Savior. One morning during prayer meeting with the camp staff, Joyce asked for prayer about her need for a co-worker. During the prayers the Lord burdened me so heavily about working with her that I could not hold back the tears. As soon as the meeting was over, I told her that I was willing to help her. She hugged me and expressed her thankfulness. But Satan would not accept defeat so easily.

A promise I had made to my mother was also causing me some distress. I had told her that as soon as I graduated from college,

I would start working and would help her with finances. Daddy had left by that time, and Mom still had two children at home and Christine in college. Mom told me to do whatever I felt God wanted me to do, but I didn't like going back on my promise. So I wrote to Miss Garrett, telling her that I had changed my mind, and I applied for a teaching position.

Unfortunately (or perhaps it was fortunate, for it added to my misery), the school to which I was assigned was a very difficult one. Well, "impossible" might be a better word. I was the only teacher, and there were eight grades. I was still a very little person, and some of the eighth grade boys were bigger than I was. That didn't make discipline very easy. In spite of the fact that I had teacher training at Caney, I found that I knew very little about teaching. Trying to keep all the students busy at the same time was very frustrating, and I was well aware that I was doing a very poor job. At length, the school board gave me a helper, an elderly gentleman who probably did not have more than a high school education, but who had taught school all his life. He was a far better teacher than I was.

Aside from all this, I discovered that I didn't really like teaching the lower grades, and I'm no good at all with discipline. Finally, I came down with a dilly of a case of influenza. That was the last straw. I quit and went home. By this time I knew perfectly well that I had disobeyed the Lord, and there was only one thing to do. What a relief when Miss Garrett came to get me, and I surrendered to God's will. The boyfriend and I soon realized the inevitable and the relationship ended. I am happy to say that he married a very lovely lady and did continue serving the Lord the rest of his life.

The rest of that year was very happy. I started visiting schools with Miss Garrett immediately. We visited about fifteen schools in a two-week cycle and did about twenty presentations. As soon as Miss Garrett finished the cycle she started, I began telling the Bible story, and she went back to doing the music as she had done with Alta Miller (now Hillegas). In between schools, she coached me on the points I had wrong or things that needed to be added. It was a wonderful way to learn. I was not called a "Bible woman" as all the others in all the districts were called. I was "the Bible girl." That was fine with me.

It was especially gratifying to go back to the Hollybush School and be the one telling the story. We had about four students from that school who went to camp that year. Some were from homes where only a few years earlier the parents would not have allowed them to go. I knew it was now allowed because my mother had dared to pave the way.

The school year was soon over, and it was camp time again. I was once again a counselor. I enjoyed helping the little girls under my care. Part of the time I lived in a counselor's room with Anna Sue Darkes. What a privilege to learn from such a godly woman. How she prayed for the girls and took every opportunity to win them to Christ. I was thoroughly convicted for my lack of interest and the shallowness of my own Christian life. Her work partner, Helen Cook, was also a great blessing. Both were great friends for many years. All the workers at Camp Nathanael were such an inspiration to me. I had much learning and growing to do, and this was just the place where I needed to be.

6

A New Challenge

"Show me the way, not to fortune and fame,
Not how to win laurels or praise for my name
But show me the way to spread the great story
That Thine is the kingdom and power and glory."

HELEN STEINER RICE

Working with Joyce Garrett in the school year of 1953–1954 also included helping in the Hardburly Community Church where Rev. Lee Hanameyer was pastor. There was a ladies Bible class, which Joyce sometimes taught, and a young people's service called the J.I.M. (Jesus is Mine) club, which Joyce taught. There was also a Wednesday night prayer meeting where I met and prayed with a group of teenage girls. I enjoyed all these services and learned so much. It was pure joy being a part of a church since I had never been actively involved before. Lajena Barker, her sister, Eleanor, and their parents also attended that church, often providing beautiful music for many of the services.

At one time the Lord put it into my heart that the young people needed something challenging to do. So I asked them to help me visit all the homes in Hardburly. Three or four girls were willing to be my helpers. We met at the church every Saturday morning for prayer, after which we started on our hike up the mountain. Hardburly was a coal mining town built on the mountainside. Margaret Sproul, another godly missionary with Scripture Memory Mountain Mission, heard of our project and gave me some good advice.

"Always pray before you leave the home," she said, "Many times that is when people soften and are more willing to listen to what God wants them to hear." So we did this.

But it was very discouraging work. Many people would very sincerely promise that they would come to church the next Sunday but never came. However, the project was not a failure. It was good training for me and for the young people. It took a lot of courage to knock on doors and invite people to church and to ask them about their soul's need. It also gave me insight into the hardness of hearts and the great need for intercessory prayer.

❖ ❖ ❖

One Sunday, not long after we visited every home in Hardburly, Pastor Hanameyer preached a sermon on *The Feeding of the Five Thousand,* from John 6:5–13. He explained the story about the little boy with the five loaves and two fish, of how Jesus prayed and then broke the bread and the fish, performing a miracle as he did so. Pastor Hanameyer then read these words, "He distributed to the disciples, and the disciples to them that were sitting down." Fourteen words, so full of meaning!

Pastor Hanameyer proceeded to ask, "Do you suppose the disciples gave food to the first few rows, gave *more* food to the first few rows, then perhaps for a third time gave even *more* food to the first few rows, and left the back rows hungry?" Pastor related this to the many areas of the world where the gospel has not been heard.

"How can we leave millions in the world hungry for the Word of God while we stuff ourselves with God's goodness?" he asked. Continuing he said, "Mark 6:42, relating the same story, says, 'They *all* ate and were satisfied.' And 2 Peter 3:9 tells us, 'The Lord is . . . not wishing for any to perish but for all to come to repentance.' Can we be any less caring?"

I thought of all those homes we visited. Only one man came down to church, and only one time. It was not the first time they were visited or invited to church. The church was in sight of every home. The houses were built on the hillside like the bleachers of a football stadium, with the church and the town businesses down on the "playing field." The whole town heard the church bell ring every Sunday. Here was a gospel witness in their midst, and they would not even come down to hear. What about those "back rows" who had not heard *even once?*

I was still thinking about the sermon on the way home. Apparently, Miss Garrett was also. About halfway home, she turned to me and said, "If I were twenty, I think I'd be on my way to the mission field!" Well I was twenty, and I was so deep in thought that I didn't even notice that the remark had been meant for me. But I answered—I don't remember if it was aloud or just to myself—"Well I *am* twenty, and I just might go!"

I couldn't forget that message. I kept pondering about those lost souls who had never heard and asking God what He wanted me to do. I was only one little girl from Hollybush. What could I do? But I knew God was a great God and could accomplish His will even through me if He so desired.

❖ ❖ ❖

Later in the year, the men's quartet from the Appalachian Bible Institute, along with Cal Beukema, a faculty member and friend of

Miss Garrett's, came to have a weekend of meetings at the church. It was planned that they would have several meals at our house. However, the night before they came, we had a terrific snowstorm. Many of the electric wires were broken, and the electricity was off in many homes, including ours. Our stove was electric. How could we cook for five men with no stove?

Well, we had one open fire place, the type with iron grating which held the fire and which was hung onto the sides of the chimney, leaving a space below for the ashes. We had this type of fireplace in Hollybush, and my mother often prepared meals on it. Mom had also roasted potatoes in the hot coals underneath the fire. Corn bread was very delicious when baked in an iron skillet under the fire. Hot coals would be knocked down from the grating, and the skillet would be placed on top of these coals. So I suggested we fry hamburgers in an iron skillet on top of the fire and roast potatoes underneath.

"And maybe we could heat a vegetable on top of the oil heater in the bedroom," Miss Garrett suggested, getting into the spirit of our improvising. That's what we did. For dessert, we made banana pudding and put it out in the snow to keep it cold since, of course, the refrigerator was not working either. The men arrived in spite of slippery roads, and we figured out ways to keep them fed.

My resourcefulness greatly impressed Miss Garrett. "My, wouldn't you do well on the mission field," she exclaimed. This time I was well aware of the implications of her remark but also realized it was true. I was raised in a somewhat primitive way, and no doubt, this would be helpful on a mission field where there were no electric (or gas) stoves or refrigerators.

These men also helped bring about another big change in both our lives. They talked a great deal about the Appalachian Bible Institute. It was a very small school, about twenty-five students, and only in its fourth year of existence. The school had need of a Dean of Women and Registrar. This was directed toward Miss Garrett.

"And you could teach English and help in other ways," they told me. I had no desire to teach anything after my experiences, but I *was* interested in learning more about God's Word. My work in the schools had opened my eyes to the fact that I still knew very little about the Bible, so I was *very* interested in becoming a student. But we gave them no answers just then.

Summer came and we went back to camp. Joyce usually did the music, playing her accordion and flashing her wonderful smile. She was also dining room hostess and many other things. I was sometimes a counselor and sometimes worked in the kitchen. Christine was there too, often helping in the kitchen as well. We became good friends with the head cook, Elresa Richert. She was so easy to work for—always making everything fun. She seemed to always notice when someone had been doing a standing job too long. She would bring over something that could be done sitting and a chair, saying, "Here, you need a sitting-down job."

We also became good friends with Nancy Johnson, SMMM's only black missionary. Nancy often worked in the kitchen with us. She was a lot of fun, and there was often much laughing while we worked. She was from Harlan, Kentucky, where there was a large population of African Americans. Her work was the same as Joyce's and mine, but in black schools. In those days, camp for black children was a separate week, and Nancy was a counselor during that week only. It was just the way things were, and I didn't think much about it. But I learned a lot about racism through my friendship with Nancy.

One day I needed to go to my mother's home. She lived in the town of Hindman at that time. I had no car, but Nancy had one and offered to take me. Christine and some other friends went along. It was only about a half-hour trip, but the day was hot and we were thirsty. Someone suggested we stop in town and get a cold drink. We talked and laughed as all of us walked into the restaurant, went to a table, and sat down—except Nancy. She kept walking around and tried to look casual. "Come sit down, Nancy," I said, totally unaware of the reason she hadn't already.

She came closer and whispered, "I can't sit down here."

"Sure you can," I said, beginning to realize what she meant. The waitress came over just then. "She can sit here with us, can't she?" I asked. We seldom had any black people in our little town, so I think the waitress was as naive as I was.

She glanced around the room, perhaps looking for her boss. Not seeing him, she answered with a shrug, "As far as I know!" Nancy sat down but kept exclaiming about how her family and friends would never believe that she sat in a restaurant and had a soda with a group of white ladies.

As Christine and I got to know Nancy better, she told us more about the discrimination she and her family endured—even when she was in Bible college, singing in the choir. When the choir went on tour she could not eat in restaurants with the other members (the restaurant's rules—not the college's). Usually several students would order her a meal along with theirs and come back to the bus to eat with her. I was appalled and saddened. What difference could the color of skin possibly make? I'm so glad America has made good progress, though I know that there is still racism.

❖ ❖ ❖

That summer SMMM invited me to officially join their organization. The Mission and Camp Nathanael, and all the other missionaries had been such a blessing to me, and I enjoyed the work. I prayed much about their invitation. One day I took my Bible and went out to the outdoor chapel. I prayed, asking God to guide me and to show me His will. Should I join SMMM or did He have something else for me? I read several portions of Scripture and prayed some more. I repeated the process several times. I received no answer. I was very confused. Fortunately the mission gave me plenty of time to make the decision.

Sometime later, in a morning chapel service, a missionary from Africa showed us slides. He talked about the needs in Africa and about areas that had never heard the gospel. It was then I heard my answer. It was as clear as if God had spoken audibly, "I want you to be a foreign missionary." I knew this was it. This was what God wanted me to do.

I talked to Joyce about it and told the mission that God had called me to the foreign field. They understood. By that time, Joyce had received a formal invitation from Appalachian Bible Institute and had already decided to accept it. Eventually I decided to go with her—as a student. It became clear to me that if I wanted to be a missionary, I needed to know the Bible better. ABI seemed to be a good place to learn.

When camp was over we began packing. Many people in our community invited us to their homes for meals. Joyce had worked in Kentucky several years and made lots of friends. Her co-workers also would miss her. We visited several of them too, saying our good-byes. I'm sure it was hard for Joyce to leave, but she was beginning to have back trouble from carrying her accordion so much. She was also carrying the responsibility for our finances. I had no income and could not help as Alta Miller had done. There were many other reasons, but the main one was that God was leading both of us to the Appalachian Bible Institute.

❖ ❖ ❖

My family was going in many different directions. Ivallean became a nurse midwife and later became a Nurse Practioner. She and Evelyn Mottram moved into a house near the high school on Caney. They delivered babies and provided prenatal and postnatal care for many women and babies in the surrounding areas. If they encountered problems, doctors were near and worked in cooperation with them.

Arlene worked as a school teacher for a while then married and moved to Michigan. In an attempt to save the marriage, Mom also moved to Michigan where Dad worked for the Chrysler Corporation, taking Chad and Priscilla with her. They moved in with Arlene and her husband, but it was not a good situation. Even though Daddy asked her to come, it was already too late. After less than a year, Mom moved back home to Hollybush, and the marriage was over. Daddy was already living with another woman. Later, Mom moved to Hindman, and the farm was eventually sold.

Christine was still at Caney during the time Mom was in Michigan and felt very alone.

7

A New Experience

"Praise the Lord! Praise God in His sanctuary; Praise Him
in His mighty expanse. Praise Him for his mighty deeds;
praise Him according to His excellent greatness."

PSALM 150:1–2

"O magnify the Lord with me, and let us exalt His name
together."

PSALM 34:3

Joyce Garrett and I arrived at the Appalachian Bible Institute a few
weeks before the students were to arrive for the new school year of
1954–1955. Joyce was given a large room in the girls' dorm, which
was the largest building on campus. It was built of cinder block and
painted blue, thus earning the label "The Blue Goose." The room
had its own bathroom but that was all. No living room, kitchen,
or storage area. We started immediately helping with the cleaning
and general preparation of the other buildings. They consisted of a
cinder block office building, near the girls' dorm, and another cinder

block construction, which housed the dining room and kitchen on the first floor and the men's dorm upstairs. This was about a block away and on the opposite side of the road. That was it, other than a few faculty homes! Classes were held in the Independent Baptist Church of Pettus, too far away for walking, so the students rode back and forth in a big blue bus.

For a few days, Joyce and I took our meals with the school's president, Dr. Lester Pipkin, and his wife Gretchen, until Mrs. Carrie "Cookie" King arrived to take over the school kitchen. My job then became helping Cookie prepare the meals, and eventually I did the cooking on her day off. I loved to cook. I learned country cooking from my mother. I learned about cooking for large groups from Elresa Richert at Camp Nathanael, and Joyce taught me a great deal in the year I was with her. She was a great cook!

I loved Cookie from the day I met her. She was short and round with grey hair and gold-rimmed glasses. Even though she was probably in her late sixties, it didn't hinder her from working long hours and producing great meals. This was the school's fifth year of existence, so there were only about forty-five students. Therefore cooking was not as big a job as it would have been for a larger school.

I stayed with Joyce until some of the students started to arrive, then I moved to student quarters in the same building.

One day we heard that a student named Austin Lockhart was arriving. He played football in high school and had chosen to come to Appalachian rather than accept a football scholarship from some much larger colleges.

I was intrigued. That was not a small thing. I learned later that he loved football and had been a good player and captain of his team. His family could not afford to send him to college, so a scholarship would have been a tremendous help. Still, he chose to attend a Bible school because God had already spoken to him about becoming a missionary.

When he arrived, I saw that he was a big strong-looking man with brown wavy hair and a ruddy complexion. He was fun-loving, always teasing and laughing. In addition, I thought that "Lorrie Lockhart" would be a beautiful, musical-sounding name! But there were several nice young men at ABI, and I was far from ready to make any serious choice.

How different the Bible institute was from Bryan College! Bryan had about three hundred students. ABI was much smaller, so I felt more at home. No one made fun of the way I talked. Most of them talked the same way. I was also, for the first time in my schooling years, about the same age as most of the other students. However, most of them came straight from high school. A few had trained elsewhere and were a bit older. I found classes easier also. I had learned more about the Bible in my two years at Bryan College and in my year with Joyce. Now I was more on the level of the other students.

I thoroughly enjoyed my classes and worked hard, studying Bible doctrine, various books of the Bible, and even Old Testament Greek, though I was the only girl in the class. I thought it might help me in learning a new language, as well as help with translation should I ever need to do that. I sang in the choir and later in a trio. I became very involved in everything and loved it all.

Classes were held only in the mornings. We came home in the big blue bus in time for lunch. Afternoons were spent studying and doing our chores.

Tuition for that first year was very small. I had come to the school not knowing how I would pay my monthly bills, but I knew God would provide. I soon learned that I could do some substitute teaching in the public schools, and that two or three days a month would cover my bills. Appalachian allowed me to do this as long as

I kept my grades up. But once again I found that I didn't do a very good job. Many students were bigger than I, and I have never been good at discipline and keeping order. I hated it. But I stuck with it as long as I could since I didn't have any other way of meeting my expenses.

Every student was required to be in the choir, though we had one young man who was a monotone. Unfortunately Austin was put in the tenor section. I think if he had been asked to sing bass, he would have done well. His voice was definitely too low for tenor. The second year not everyone was required to join, so he and the monotone dropped out. As for me, I loved singing. I had taken a few lessons at Bryan, but I didn't do well as a soloist. At ABI I found I could do better in duets or trios.

My second year the soprano in the main trio did not return to school, and I took her place. We often traveled with Dr. Pipkin and sang before his messages. It was a magical time, and I was happier than I had ever been in my life.

One weekend the trio and Dr. Pipkin went to my home area, to the Ivis Bible Church, which was having a homecoming. It was a hot summer day, and the windows were open. The trio was up front singing when I saw—and heard—the audience gasp. I didn't know why. We just kept singing. Afterward I learned that a fly had flown right into the alto's mouth and there was nothing she could do but swallow and keep on singing! Our choir director, Cal Beukema, always told us, "If the house burns down around you, keep your eyes on me and keep singing." We certainly acted in the spirit of that admonition that day.

A very special event occurred the winter of my first year. The whole student body went to Chicago to the Moody Bible Institute to attend the Moody Founder's Week Conference. We stayed in the dormitories with the Moody students. Some morning meetings were held in the school auditorium, but in the evening we walked to the Moody Church for the meetings. It was so cold. We had not been allowed to date in West Virginia, but while in Chicago we were allowed to have two dates. Austin (his family and friends called him Audy) did ask me for a date, but I had already met my quota and couldn't accept. Still, I was very pleased that he asked.

The meetings were very challenging, and the time spent in the cars driving up to Chicago and back to the school helped us get to know some of the faculty better. I remember some deep discussions on theology. Some of the faculty disagreed on some points of doctrine, and it helped me to form my own beliefs by hearing different sides discussed.

❖ ❖ ❖

Lots of dedicated people came to speak in chapel and sometimes in classes. Most of these stirred my heart to dedicate myself more fully to serving our great God. But no one stirred me more than Mr. and Mrs. Lehman Keener. They were with The Unevangelized Fields Mission (now called Crossworld). They talked about a country called Dutch New Guinea, where UFM was just beginning a work.

Dutch New Guinea was a very primitive country. The native people didn't even wear clothing—just a small bit of covering made of grass or bamboo. It was also very dangerous. There was constant warfare among the different tribes, and they were not friendly toward strangers. I thought about Pastor Lee Hanameyer's sermon about those neglected "back rows." The people of New Guinea had probably *never* heard the good news of salvation, and if anyone in the world needed the gospel, they did. I really wanted to go there. But when I expressed my thoughts to the Keeners, they told me UFM decided it was too dangerous for single girls, only couples or single men could go. I was terribly disappointed.

I constantly prayed, asking God for guidance. I definitely wanted to go to a place where the people had rarely or never heard the gospel. Some countries in South America, especially Peru, seemed very needy. UFM had work in Brazil, Guyana, and other small countries which also seemed in the "unreached" category. I soon became fairly settled on UFM, but not on a particular country. But I couldn't get Dutch New Guinea out of my head or my heart.

❖ ❖ ❖

The student body at Appalachian was so small that we grew to know everyone well and really became a family. I learned from other students as well as from the faculty. Of all my years of schooling both before and after, the two years I spent at ABI were the most enjoyable and brought about the most life-changing events for me. I made many friends. Some who now flash on my memory screen are: Betty Kemper, the alto of the trio I was in, (the one who swallowed the fly) who was always singing and with whom I worked for a year after graduating; Lillian Wegner, one of the many Wegners who attended ABI, who also sang with me in the trio; Mary Gall, my first roommate, taught me so much about dedication. There were many others.

Austin Lockhart became one of those special friends. He had been saved less than two years, yet he demonstrated a deep love for God. His prayers were so sincere, I found myself marveling that one so young in the faith seemed so comfortable in God's presence. I listened more intently when he prayed.

Christine attended Bryan University but was having a hard time, as I had my first year there. She had attended Caney Junior College for her first two years of college, and when Mom moved to Michigan she felt very alone. Going farther away from home to Bryan, which is in Dayton, Tennessee, made matters even worse. So she decided to come to Appalachian with me when I returned for my second year. It was good having her there. Settling into the family atmosphere, she soon became happier. She was well-liked and developed many friendships. She was so pretty with her dark, naturally curly hair and olive skin. She was also tall and slender. We didn't really look like sisters, but we were always close.

The second year dating was allowed for special, school-planned events. The first date I had with Austin was a trip for the whole student body, to Charleston for a Youth for Christ meeting. He told me on that first date that I was the kind of girl he wanted to marry someday. I was flattered but a bit put off as well. This was much too soon to talk of such things. I did enjoy being with him, though, and we soon began dating fairly regularly.

Part of the year he and I were both on the planning committee for the school socials, so it was easy for us to go together. He was so much fun. I could tell that Joyce liked him too, and that was important to me. He was interested in going to the mission field and had been challenged to go to a country where men were especially needed.

All of that was wonderful. But I was very unsure, and I did give him a hard time with my on-again, off-again actions. I wanted to be absolutely sure of God's leading for my future, and I didn't trust my own emotions. I broke up with him once just because I was so unsure. During that time another girl who was very beautiful started giving him a lot of attention and awakened a bit of jealousy in me.

My good friend Cookie King told me she was very irritated when she saw this girl "batting her eyes at him." I laughed but hoped he would not fall for such a ploy. She was on the same team with Audy for their Christian Service assignment, so one night he called her about the assignment. When she came back to the room where I was, she said, "Guess who that was on the phone?"

"Who was it?" I asked, deciding to play along.

When she told me it was Audy, I said, "Oh, what did he want?" Then she answered, "Oh, I don't know; I guess he just wanted to say good night!" I didn't believe her, and Audy and I laughed about it later.

One day a group of girls gathered in one of the rooms just talking and having fun when the dorm phone rang, and someone called up the stairs saying it was for me. It was Audy. He asked if I would go with him to a Youth for Christ meeting in Huntington, and would I sing? I said yes without hesitation. As soon as I hung up, I ran back up to where all the girls were gathered and started dancing around the room.

"What's the matter with her? Who called her?" etc., the girls kept asking each other. Finally I sat down and told them Audy had asked me for a date. So we were back together. It was a wonderful trip to Huntington. He was giving a testimony and did such a good job that when I got up to sing, I felt I couldn't spoil it by getting nervous as I often did. This time I sang with my heart, and I did okay.

Toward the end of the second year, Audy asked me what was going to happen with us when the school year finished. Without doing much thinking, I answered, "Well, I guess we'll just go our separate ways."

His answer was totally unexpected, "Well then, I think we should just break up now." Wow! I was so shocked and sorry I had spoken so hastily. We said good night, and I went to my room and began to cry. I cried off and on for the next several days. I really didn't want to go our separate ways. In fact, the thought of never seeing him again was almost unbearable. Maybe Audy knew his declaration would force me to face the question more realistically. I think he knew long before I did that I loved him, and he kept patiently waiting for me to come to that conclusion.

❖ ❖ ❖

Changes were taking place at the school. God provided a large plot of land in Bradley, West Virginia, a former dairy farm, for the Appalachian Bible College. There was enough acreage for many years of expansion. But there was only one usable building on the property, a small Cape Cod style home and one chicken coop! Yes, that's what it had been, but it could be remodeled, and was later used for housing for married students.

One day the whole student body went up to the new property, about two hours away. We cleaned and painted. The men cleared land, anything that would be helpful when the school moved. It was a nice outing, a break from classes for us. Work began on the new all-purpose building in April of 1955.

There was a Junior-Senior banquet about a month before graduation. Audy and I did not go together, but he sat in the seat behind me on the bus. We talked the whole way to the banquet site. That encouraged me, and when I got the chance, I secretly switched my name card with another girl so I could sit across the table from him!

The junior class collected baby pictures of each graduate, which they showed on a screen, and people were asked to guess who it was. I was sure they didn't have one of me. To my knowledge only one existed, and it was with my two older sisters. But there it was, cropped from that picture. Audy laughed with glee at the look on my face when the picture appeared. It was a wonderful evening.

Then it was time for graduation. There were only ten of us. It was the last graduation at that location. ABI moved that summer to Bradley, West Virginia. It was a great service. Mrs. Pipkin played a piano medley of each graduate's favorite hymn. My hymn was "I Am His and He is Mine." I knew whatever happened in the future that I would always belong to my wonderful Lord, and I would be content in serving Him, even if it was without Austin. But, hallelujah, that wasn't God's plan!

After the graduation service, the female graduates went into a room to remove our gowns, touch up makeup, etc. Someone knocked on the door, and I answered. Audy was standing there smiling at me. "I have borrowed Johnny's car," he said. "I can take you to the school for the party." He didn't actually ask, but asking wasn't necessary. I was more than happy to go with him. I felt like I could go dancing around the room again, like the song, "I could have danced all night." I didn't. But I sure enjoyed the wonderful graduation party.

Some former graduates returned for the graduation of their friends. One of those was Don Crisp, who graduated the previous year. He and I had been friends and sang some duets together. He lived in Martin, Kentucky, near my home, so he offered to take Christine and me home. I planned to stay at the school to work for a while, so I thanked him and declined but suggested that Christine would probably like a ride. She had only met him once before. She was with me for part of the weekend when the quartet visited the Hardburly Church. (Don was the tenor in the quartet.) But they immediately felt very comfortable with each other.

On the trip home they talked, sang, and generally got acquainted. By the time they reached my mother's home (about a three-hour trip), they both decided in their hearts that they would marry each other. And after only three months of dating they did just that. After more than fifty years, they are still singing and serving the Lord together.

Audy took me home after I finished my work and met my mother and sister Priscilla. He returned to the school and spent the summer working on the all-purpose building at the new location.

I had kept contact with UFM since meeting Mr. and Mrs. Keener. The mission suggested that I take a course at the Summer Institute of Linguistics in Norman, Oklahoma. Joyce offered to pay for my trip to Oklahoma and gave me the choice of going by bus, by train, or flying. I think she was disappointed that I chose to fly. It was the most expensive. But I had never been on a train and was a bit afraid of not knowing how to cope with all the details. A bus would be a long tiring trip, and as I found out later, it wasn't a very safe way to travel.

It was an interesting summer. We studied ways to learn a new language. Native Americans who spoke different languages were brought in to help us. We learned phonetics and how to record the different sounds and phonemics, how to learn different grammatical structures, and much more. We lived in some of the University of Oklahoma dorms that were not air conditioned. It was hot—over 100 degrees much of the time! But we survived, and the training was very helpful when we reached New Guinea.

❖ ❖ ❖

By this time Mom was living in Hindman, Kentucky. Her marriage was over, though there was not a formal divorce for a few more years. Daddy stayed in Michigan and moved in with a woman named Ann. He lived with her for several years until she died of cancer. They never married.

I didn't see or hear from my father for several years. He had been away from home so much already, and I had been away at school, so it didn't affect me much. Others, however, especially my mother, suffered greatly. She was now without any means of support, and Chad and Priscilla were still at home. Mom did some babysitting and took care of an elderly woman for a while, but that income was not nearly enough to provide their needs.

My sister Ivy, who was working as a public health nurse, helped her as much as she could. As soon as Chad was old enough, he enlisted in the Air Force. His allotment provided for Mom and Priscilla to at least have their basic needs met. Later, Ivy bought a house for them, and Mom lived there until her death in 1988. Priscilla eventually became a nurse and worked in a hospital in Michigan for many years.

8

Satan Strikes

"The Lord is my rock and my fortress and my deliverer;
My God, my rock, in whom I take refuge; my shield and
the horn of my salvation, my stronghold."

PSALM 18:2

When the linguistics course was nearly finished, I had to find a way to get home. Friends from Bryan University, Ralph and Melba Maynard, who also attended the linguistics course, were willing to take me to Indianapolis, but I would have to take a bus from there. I was not happy to have to ride a bus, but it seemed my best option.

We left Oklahoma late in the day and had to spend a night in a hotel. They got a room and had a cot put in for me in a slightly separate area. I didn't help with paying for the room or for gas for the car. It embarrasses me even today that I didn't, but I had barely enough money for the bus. They said nothing and were very kind and helpful to me.

Ralph and Mel took me to a bus station in Indianapolis, and I boarded a bus for Lexington, Kentucky. It was already evening, and

I rode all night, sleeping very little. The bus arrived in Lexington in the wee hours of the morning. I immediately went to the desk and asked when the next bus was due going to Hazard. That was as close as I could get to home. From there I would have to get a taxi or call someone to come and get me.

I was shocked and devastated when I was told, "Not until four o'clock this afternoon!" It was then about four o'clock in the morning. I had traveled for almost two days, had very little sleep, and I would have to wait around in the bus station for about twelve hours! I felt like crying.

I had turned to go find a seat when a man in his late forties or early fifties approached me. He held a cup of coffee and looked a bit sleepy, as most of the people in the bus station looked. He was unshaven and a bit unkempt, but I had seen my daddy look like that at the end of a long hard work day.

"Ma'am," he said, "I overheard what was said about the bus. I live in Hazard, but I work in Ohio. I'm on my way home, just stopped in here to get a cup of coffee." Such a plausible story, such a kind sounding voice, but, unknown to me then, such a wicked heart! Mom had always told us never to accept a ride from a stranger. I knew better. But I was so tired and had such a long wait ahead of me, his words were very enticing. "You'd be welcome to ride with me," he said, "and if you're not comfortable with going alone, maybe there would be someone else who would want to go with you. Go ahead and ask around if you want."

I said, "Well, I could ask." I'm sure he already knew that no one would be there that early waiting to go to Hazard. He continued to be so kind and understanding about my reluctance. And he did seem like such a harmless man. I finally said "Yes," I would go. It was a terribly wrong decision, and I only tell this story in the hope that it will help some other young lady to make a better choice.

This man—I never knew his name—continued to be kind until we were in his car and on our way. Then he suddenly asked, "Have you ever been with a man?" My heart started pounding. I knew immediately that I was in serious trouble. At first I pretended I didn't know what he meant. "I have a boyfriend," I said, "and we go places together."

"I mean, have you ever *been* with a man," he said with great irritation.

"No," I answered. "I'm a Christian, and I wouldn't until I'm married."

"I don't believe you," he said harshly and started driving faster.

My mind also started racing, *What am I going I do? I need to get out of this car!* I tried to stay calm. I didn't want to anger him. I did my best to talk to him about God. He ignored me and started driving even faster. I was afraid to try to jump out of the car. I prayed desperately for God to help me out of this predicament that I had foolishly gotten myself into. Soon we were on a country road. I had watched the signs and knew we were on the road to Hazard, and that it would be country most of the way. *Maybe when he slows down for a curve, I could jump out. Lord, help me!*

Questions were tangled with my frantic prayers. Was this going to be the end of my plans to become a missionary? God had helped me all along the way, providing guidance, finances, and all that was needed through all those years of education. Was it now going to end because of this one foolish decision? Was my life itself going to end?

Suddenly he pulled off the road, down a leaf-covered path. And I froze. I couldn't move. I had never heard of a simple rape, only combination rape and murder. Maybe in those days it just wasn't talked about. But I fully expected that he would kill me. I also thought that it probably would be futile to try to run away. He could chase me down or hit me with the car. I was more scared than I had ever been in my life.

It was so early in the morning that almost no cars were on the road. There was no use screaming for help, no one could hear. He stopped the car and started talking again—things I can't repeat. He then started to force me down on the car seats. I fought as hard as I could. I know that today sometimes victims are advised not to fight, but I couldn't *not* fight.

I did have a fleeting thought that maybe if I gave in, he wouldn't kill me. But my second thought was that I'd rather die than submit. Of course he was stronger than I and soon did force me down, and got on top of me. He tried to kiss me, but I tucked my lips inside my mouth and clamped down hard. He was *not* going to kiss my lips!

When he discovered that I was indeed a virgin, he unbelievably (*miraculously*) let me up, and he stepped outside the car. As the cold morning air came in, I started shaking. I didn't cry. I think I was just too scared.

When he got back in the car, his attitude was totally different again. "You're cold," he said kindly. "Come sit here close to me. I promise I won't bother you." But I couldn't. I sat as close to the door as I could—and shook. I turned my head and looked out the window.

Through the hazy morning light I could just see the idyllic setting. A small stream was just a few feet from where we were parked. Just beyond that was a large meadow and a farm house on the far side, with smoke curling out of the chimney. So close and yet so unreachable. So peaceful, in stark contrast to the turmoil and horror of what was happening to me. He started the car and began to turn around. But I was in for another shock.

Suddenly from under some clothes and blankets in the back seat, a younger man sat up. I was so startled I could hardly breathe. *Oh no,*

I thought. *I'm going to have to go through this all over again. Please, Lord, No!* I had been totally unaware that anyone else was in the car.

"Where are we?" the young man asked.

"We're on our way to Hazard," the older man said.

"Hazard? Why are we going to Hazard?" asked the young man.

"We're taking this young lady," he answered, "and don't you bother her, she's a good girl."

He pulled the car back onto the road and continued toward Hazard. But when we came to a little diner beside the road, he said to me. "You need some coffee and some breakfast." So all three of us went into the restaurant and had breakfast. The coffee **was** good and hot and I did eat a little because I was very hungry. I hadn't eaten since noon the previous day. It seemed so bizarre to be eating breakfast with these men as if nothing was wrong.

When we got back in the car the young man drove, and the older man got in the back seat. I decided these two men were going to hear the gospel whether they wanted to hear it or not. I didn't care if they thought I was a complete religious nut or anything else. My Bible was in a little case which at my feet. I got it out and asked if they would mind if I read out loud. They probably were so stunned that they didn't know what else to say but "no." I started reading at the third chapter of John and read several chapters. There was complete silence when I finished.

I then started asking them to drop me off at the next bus station. I didn't know if I would still have to wait until the four o'clock bus came along, but anything was better than being in the car with these two men, and I now knew that neither of them lived in Hazard. They dropped me off at a tiny little store and bus stop. They carried my suitcases in and started to go. I said to the older man, "Please, never do this to anyone else." He didn't answer. He left, then came back in and asked me for money for gas! I think I gave him two dollars. I figured it was the quickest way to have them gone.

My dilemma now was how to get home, and now more than ever I desperately wanted to get there. I went over to the man behind the counter. I must have looked absolutely awful, and I wonder what he thought about the situation. I asked about a bus and was told there was nothing until about five o'clock – the same one leaving Lexington at four. "But," he continued, "in about half an hour a taxi should arrive. He usually parks right over there," pointing to a wide area beside the road.

When the taxi arrived, I asked if he would take me all the way to Hindman for ten dollars, all I had, and he agreed. I was actually reluctant to get into the taxi with the driver but had no choice. I *had* to get home. But he was very pleasant, and I even began to relax a little.

The taxi driver wouldn't take me all the way to my mother's house, but only to the town of Hindman. After asking permission, I left my suitcases in a store and walked the rest of the way, about two miles. Mom was surprised to see me that early. I explained enough to satisfy her but told her nothing about what I had been through. I was too ashamed that I had so foolishly accepted a ride with a stranger and then had been too scared to try to get away.

I ran a hot bath and asked her if she had some kind of disinfectant I could add to the water because I "felt so dirty from the travel." She brought me some Lysol I think, and I poured quite a bit into the water. I literally scrubbed myself from head to toe, and then went to bed and slept several hours.

I didn't tell anyone what had happened for about five years. I just couldn't talk about it. I sealed it off in the back of my mind and tried to pretend that it was all just a terrible nightmare. And I did have nightmares about it for more than a year. Unfortunately, my ordeal wasn't quite over.

❖ ❖ ❖

Meanwhile Christine was getting married in just a few days. It was wonderful therapy for me to get caught up in all the planning. She wanted me to sing, so there was practicing to do. Audy and I had been writing lots of letters. He had been at the school (ABI) all summer helping in the construction of the building at the new location in Bradley. He persuaded me to let him come down for Chris and Don's wedding, which wasn't very hard to do. I was eager to see him.

When the day came, I kept watching for him. When I saw his car pull up in front of Mom's house, I ran out, and instead of waiting for him to get out of the car, I jumped in beside him. I was so glad to see him. Audy told me later that right then he knew he had me.

We talked a bit and then got out and went into the house. My sister Ivallean had come home for the wedding, and as soon as she could, she pulled me aside and said, "Now that's what I call a man. If you don't want him I'll take him!" I laughed. It made me happy that she approved. It was that evening when I *finally* realized I was very much in love with him, and that I might as well stop fighting it.

Audy was Don's best man at the wedding, and I sang my song for him as well as for Chris and Don. It was a happy time. It helped me to push my awful ordeal a bit further back, away from my conscious thoughts.

Austin and I did a lot of talking about the future. We decided that I should go ahead and go to candidate school with the Unevangelized Fields Mission, and he would go later. I would need to tell the Mission as soon as I could that, while I was not technically engaged, I did have a serious relationship, and I wanted to go to New Guinea.

So, in late August I traveled to Bala Cynwyd, Pennsylvania, for their candidate school. I have no idea how I got the money to go.

But God always provided what was needed. I was put in a room with three or four other single girls.

I started praying that God would give me an opportunity to talk to Mrs. Pudney. I thought that would be easier than trying to talk to Mr. Pudney, the director of the mission, about such a sensitive matter. I knew they would not accept me for going to New Guinea as a single girl. God answered the next morning. Just as I walked out of my room, Mrs. Pudney called to me, "Could you please come and help me make my bed?" as if she knew I needed to talk to her.

I told her I wanted to go to New Guinea, and that I expected to be getting married soon. She was very kind and understanding. "I think that can be arranged," she said. She, of course, passed on our conversation to her husband and others in leadership, and it was agreed that I could be accepted with a *'proviso'* that Austin also be accepted when he was able to attend candidate school. When I met with the Board at the end of our time there, that was how I was accepted. I returned home, not knowing what the next step would be.

❖ ❖ ❖

A short time later Dr. Pipkin called, asking me to return to Appalachian for that school year (1956–57). He wanted me to help with the public school visitation program. Austin still had one year of school, and this would enable us to see each other often. I had spent a year with Joyce Garrett doing school visitation. It was close to my heart, and I would be working with my friend, Betty Kemper, who graduated with me. So I was glad for this opportunity.

Dr. Pipkin said he would come to Kentucky in about a week in order to pick up some furniture that had been donated to ABI. He would have a student, Ron Dillon, with him, but there would be room for me. I was all packed and ready when they arrived. I had to ride in the cab of a truck between the two men, but these were very godly men, and though a little uncomfortable, I was happy to have a way of getting to the school.

All went well until we approached South Charleston, West Virginia. They picked me up in the late afternoon, and it was now dark, maybe nine or ten o'clock. Dr. Pipkin needed a break from driving, and Ron was at the wheel. I sat in the middle with Dr. Pipkin by the door. This was before Route 64 was built, and the roads were narrow and winding. We approached a railroad crossing where the road curved to the right to cross the tracks, and on up a steep incline, followed by a turn to the left.

I saw someone walking on the tracks carrying a lantern but thought nothing of it. Ron pulled onto the tracks and started to change gears for pulling up the incline, but killed the motor.

Suddenly Dr. Pipkin yelled, "Let's get out of here!" He jumped out pulling me out also, and ran up the incline dragging me with him, only stopping when he reached the top. I didn't know what was happening. Ron stayed with the truck and finally got the motor running again. And just like in the movies, the truck lunged forward off the tracks, and a railroad car went by. It was only one car, but it could have destroyed the truck—and us! It happened so fast. We had been minutes from death. The man on the tracks had obviously been trying to signal us to stop before the tracks, and fortunately Dr. Pipkin had seen the railroad car coming.

Ron pulled up the incline, made the left turn, and pulled off the road. He came walking toward us holding out the truck keys. Dr. Pipkin accepted them. We were all pretty shaken as we got back into the truck but thankful that God had spared our lives. There was much work for Him that He wanted each of us to do. The rest of the trip was uneventful, though Ron did do some driving again later.

When I went to breakfast the next morning, I found the whole school, including Audy, had already heard about our narrow escape. Audy came over and talked to me, but there was no hugging. It wasn't allowed. The smiles, however, were pretty broad.

❖ ❖ ❖

I had been at the school only a few days when I started feeling ill. The next day a big celebration was planned for the dedication of the new building. But I wasn't able to get out of bed. I had a terrible stomachache mostly on the right side. Betty went to the celebration but kept coming back to the room to check on me, and near the end of the day brought a doctor. He concluded that I had appendicitis. So I was bundled up, carried to his car, and taken to the hospital.

The doctor in the emergency room examined me, and then left the room for what seemed like a long time. I was very cold. I managed to get up, get my coat, and put it on. I sat down on a bench, leaned my head against the corner piece, and basically lost consciousness. After a while, a nurse came in and sternly ordered me to get up on the gurney she had brought. I couldn't see and was barely conscious, but she didn't offer any assistance. I have often wondered why she was so unkind. Did she know what was wrong with me and thought I didn't deserve kindness? I somehow managed to get on the gurney, and she took me to a room—actually a ward. There were about eight other patients in the room. I was put to bed and given some injections. The next morning I was better.

Later in the day a doctor came in and explained that I had an infection in the fallopian tubes. It was not appendicitis. I didn't put it all together at the time, but suspected that it *might* have had something to do with the rape. Though a lot had happened, it had only been about six weeks since the incident. More than a year later when I took a medical course in California, I recognized the symptoms and suspected that it had been a venereal disease, one that was curable with antibiotics. But no one ever told me that, and to this day, I don't know for sure. I'm just thankful that I never had any further symptoms, and I recovered fully.

Audy was allowed to come in and see me at the hospital. He brought with him a long roll of signatures and well wishes from all my friends. I was delighted. After a few days I was able to go back to the school.

Betty and I got back to school visitation. She usually did the music, and I told the story. But if there was a piano in a school, she would play, and I would lead the singing also. Sometimes she told the story. We worked well together, and we enjoyed telling the Bible stories to both children and teachers. According to an early history of ABI by Robert E. Kresge, we reached three thousand boys and girls every two weeks. It is so very sad that this is no longer allowed in public schools.

❖ ❖ ❖

For those few months, it seemed that Satan was trying to destroy me in one way or another. But, Praise God, he was allowed to go only so far and no further. I had already been set apart for God's service, and though I was small, insignificant, and ignorant of Satan's devices, I was precious to God, and He had protected me.

Also, in the midst of all the bad things that happened, God gave me peace and great joy in my relationship with Audy. I would survive and follow God in spite of Satan's attacks. It was, of course, wrong of me not to tell Audy about the rape before we married. He had a right to know. But putting it into words made it too real. I couldn't do it. I did tell him that I might have a problem having children but nothing more.

I prayed fervently and continuously that God would help me to not let my horrible experience in any way affect my relationship with Audy. About four years after we were married, I finally told him. He was very kind and loving. When I next saw my Mom, I told her and eventually my sisters and a few others. Somehow telling it took away some of the horror. Even today, more than fifty-five years later, remembering and writing it down stirs up a turmoil of emotions.

Our house on Hollybush, with Mom and Chris on the steps.

Mom and Dad in their early years.

The stone chapel at Camp Nathanael.

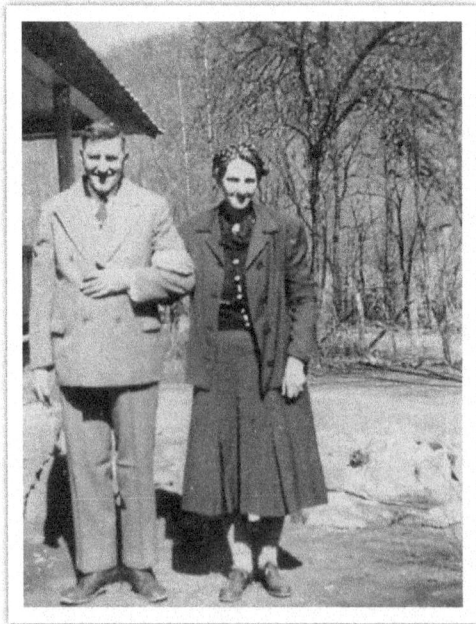

My grandparents on Mom's side, Cleveland and Vilora Huff.

My grandparents on Dad's side, Preston and Margaret Caudill.

Christine, Arlene, and Me.

Joyce Garrett with me at my graduation from Bryan University.

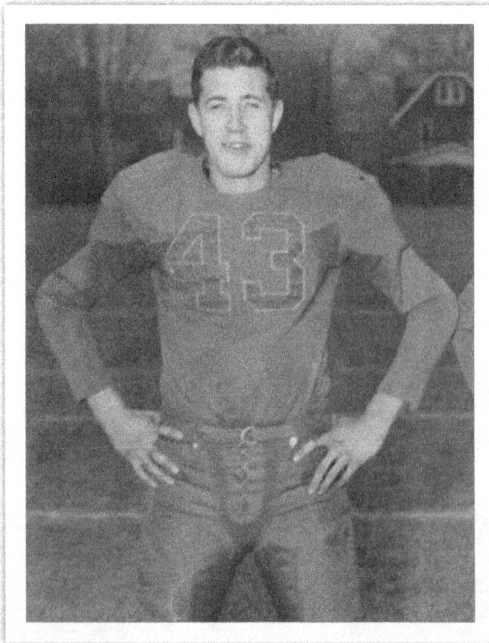

Audy Lockhart in his football uniform.

Our Wedding in 1958.

The wedding party pictured from left to right: Priscilla, Chad, Lorrie, Austin, Rev. Stevens, Christine. Friends across the back with Jennings on far right. Flower girl, Mary, on bench.

Tanimkon and Mutki with their two boys.

Church leaders at Kiwi, Okngungan and
Kapinip with Hannah (back left).

The storage building (gudang). The door on the left was the clinic.

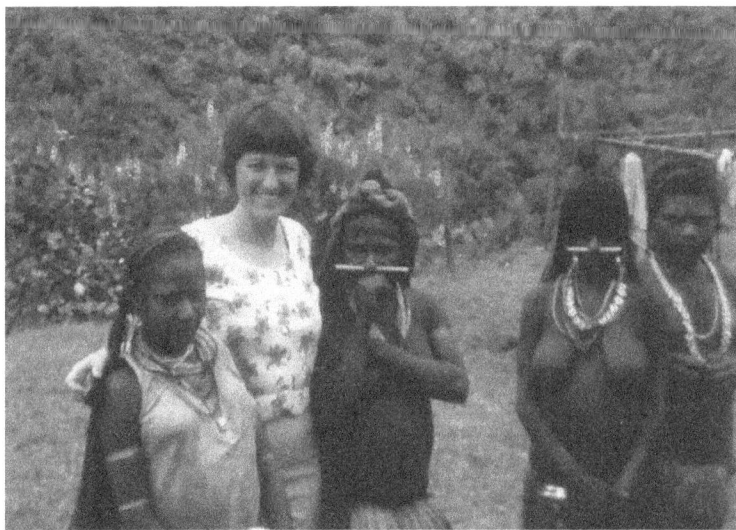

My sister Ivy with some of the Kiwi ladies.

Audy and Russ Bond ready to leave for Kiwi.

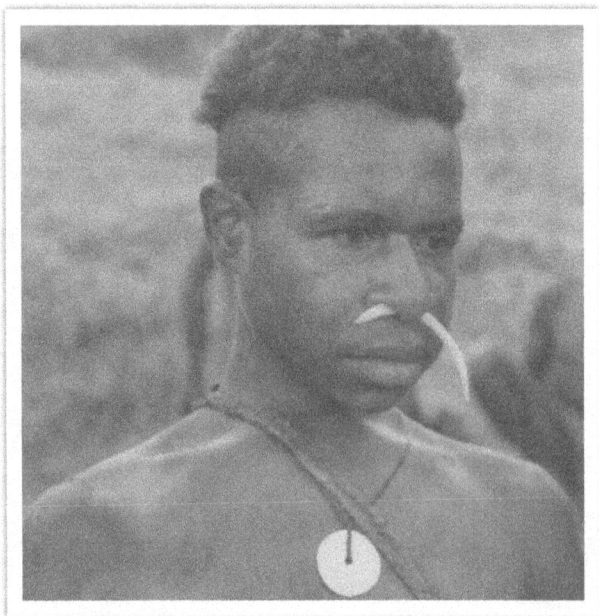

Portrait of a man with a bone piercing his septum and
a bone circle necklace.

Our daughters are ready to head off to school with
Rachael Carne and Pilot Bob Brueker.

Our family on our first furlough.
Children are pictured from left to right: Leah, Fran, Beth, Alice.

Profile of a man with a bone through his septum and a large, gauge-style ear piercing.

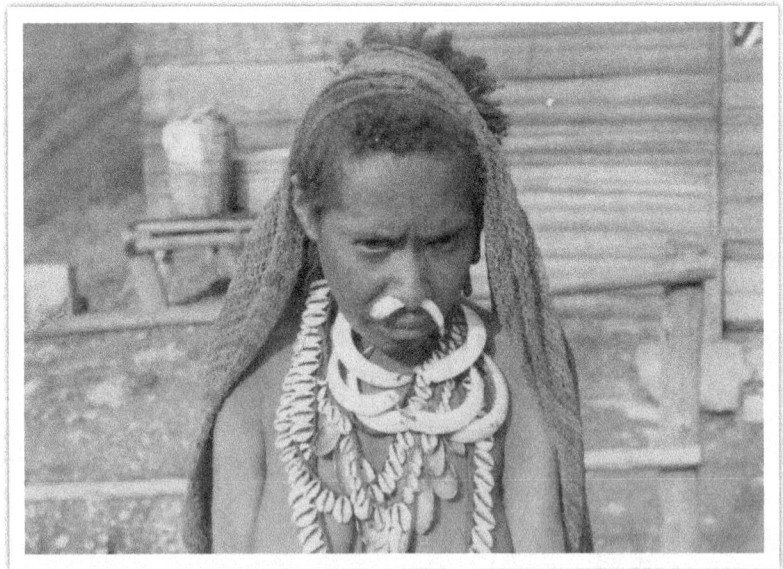

A woman wears a headdress and a large assortment of bone and shell necklaces.

My brother Chad pictured with my sister Priscilla.

My daughters in 2012 at my granddaughter Laura's wedding.
Pictured from left to right: Alice, Leah, Me, Beth, and Fran.

CHAPTER

9

Moving Forward

"How blessed is he whose help is the God of Jacob,
whose hope is in the Lord his God."

PSALM 146:5

"Let us exalt his name together."

PSALM 34:3

One day Dr. Pipkin called me into his office. "You realize," he
said, "that you are not under the student rules." Yes, I knew that.
"But, Austin is a student, and *is* under the rules." I knew that too.
I wasn't quite sure if he was saying we hadn't quite been following
the rules, or if this was just a caution. He didn't say much else, so I
was left to wonder.

One of the rules, we learned later, had caused some heated
discussion in a faculty meeting. The rule was that students could not
get married or even engaged until after they graduated.

Austin and I were definitely planning, in our own minds, to marry
each other. But because of the rule, he had not actually proposed.

This did cause us quite a dilemma. Some thought we had already broken the rule since we both planned to go to New Guinea. Yet we couldn't make any definite plans for getting married or about when we could go to New Guinea.

Some faculty members felt that students should be allowed to get engaged before graduation, and we were cited as an example of why it would be better. Others wanted the rule to remain. We heard later that our situation helped the faculty to eventually change that rule. Dr. Pipkin asked us not to discuss marriage for the rest of Audy's school year. However, there did seem to be some leniency. Even Dr. Pipkin himself publically prayed for us using both our names, asking God to guide "as they prepare to go to the mission field."

Austin had been pastoring a small church out in the country, and I was allowed to go with him every Sunday evening. One Sunday Austin asked his good friend, Jack Davis, to preach for him. Jack and his wife, Loretta, had often been our chaperones on our dates. Loretta and some of their children were with him that night. Jack was very tall, and the ceiling in the church was very low. It was winter, and the heat was a little too warm. Jack made it through his sermon and said, "Let's pray." There was complete silence for a couple of minutes and then a thud. Jack had fainted from the heat!

Audy ran to him and quickly got him to some fresh air. He was soon just fine, to the great relief of everyone. That incident was a good source of much laughing and teasing for many years.

Audy's graduating class, 1957, was small and the first one in the new location. His mother, Pauline Lockhart, sisters Linda (about 9) and Mary (about 6) and his sister-in-law, Barbara, all came up for the graduation. I was so happy to sit with the family.

After the school year finished, Betty Kemper and I worked at some Vacation Bible Schools and helped at a camp for a few weeks. It was a difficult summer for me. Chior Director Cal Beukema persuaded us to accept an invitation that had been extended to him, to conduct a VBS at the City Bible Center in Charleston, West Virginia, a large church. I had never even attended a Vacation Bible School, though I had helped a little in one or two. I knew almost nothing about how to be in charge. Again I felt so small, lacking in the experiences that many of my friends had.

Betty did almost all the work of planning and directing. I led the singing, told the serialized story, and helped where I could, but Betty definitely carried an unfair share of the work. There were a good number of well-qualified teachers and helpers, and I think it turned out okay, but no credit to me. I was really glad when the week was over.

I did better when we helped at a camp. I was much more familiar with the camp scene. We were able to take several children with us from the schools we visited. Any children who wanted to go could choose to do the Scripture memorization program like Camp Nathanael had, or they could pay for the week. We were so happy to have the opportunity to introduce these children to camp life, and in some cases to Christ, the Savior.

❖ ❖ ❖

Audy resigned his church near ABI, moved back to Huntington, and began working, trying to save some money. We saw each other when we could. He also accepted another church in Owingsville, Kentucky. It was about an hour from his home, so he could drive down on weekends and still work in Huntington. The congregation was small, but he really enjoyed getting to know the people and ministering to them.

Toward the end of the summer, I went down to Huntington to spend a few days with Audy. I usually stayed with Mr. and Mrs. Charlie Hayes, but this time, I went directly to his parent's home since it was almost time for him to come home from work. I always enjoyed spending time with his mother. She was a great lady and easy to talk to.

Audy did come home after a short while but said he had something he needed to do and left again. I was a bit hurt. Why couldn't I at least go with him?

Finally he came back, and we went for a drive. We were on Airport Road a little south of the city of Huntington, when he pulled over and parked. Turning to me and smiling, he asked, "Will you marry me?"

Wow! I hadn't expected that! After taking a deep breath and recovering my composure, I answered, "Of course I'll marry you!" Reaching around me, he opened the glove compartment and pulled out a small box—the reason for his mysterious disappearance. I could only see the ring by the light from the glove compartment, but it was definitely beautiful. He put the ring on my finger where it remains today, fifty-plus years later. I was ecstatically happy. I couldn't believe that this wonderful man wanted to spend the rest of his life with me—small, incompetent, not-too-pretty me.

The rest of that week I stayed with Audy's aunt Chris and her husband, Walter Rood. Audy and I did a lot of talking about the future. We discussed when to get married and how to proceed with getting to the mission field. UFM suggested that I take a course in missionary medicine in California—more schooling, whew!

Since we were planning to go to a very primitive country, having at least a basic knowledge of medicine would be very helpful both for our own family and for the native people. I had already applied for that. Audy would go to candidate school and then take some college courses at Marshall University in Huntington, working toward a degree sometime in the future. He would also continue working. The wedding would be put off for another year. It seemed like a lifetime to me, but we were trying to be practical, "sensible."

I went home for a few weeks but came back to Huntington nearer my departure date. After only a few days, we sadly parted, and I left for California on a bus. It was a long trip, and I was fearful, but it was all I could afford. (I think Audy actually bought my ticket for me.) I arrived at the Biola University campus early in the morning and had to wait for the doors to open. I was really, really tired.

Fortunately, one of the first people I saw was a friend from Appalachian, David Fox. He and his wife, Vivian, transferred to Biola the previous year. He worked as a night security guard. How wonderful to see a familiar face, even though later he told me that I "looked like something the cats dragged in!" When the doors opened, I was welcomed, registered, and shown my room. As soon as I could, I went to bed and slept most of the day.

Soon the other students arrived. My roommate quickly became a friend, and the others were easy to get to know. There were about twenty-five of us in the School of Missionary Medicine, and almost all of us planned to be missionaries. I really enjoyed getting to know them and hearing how God had led in their lives. I also enjoyed the studies. We learned about a lot of tropical diseases—malaria, cholera, yaws, etc. Many of these sicknesses were prevalent in New Guinea.

Nurses still wore caps in those days, and we had a capping ceremony after the first three months. We started working in a hospital after that, learning basic things, always under supervision. I liked working with the patients. I found their stories very interesting and had to watch myself so that I didn't talk too much and neglect my work.

Since this was California, I met a few famous people. Bing Crosby's sister-in-law was there in the hospital a few days. I only carried in her lunch tray. Joy Ritterhoff, the founder of the mission, Gospel Recordings, which God used in multiplying the ministry of missionaries, was my patient. I had a few good talks with her. I counted it a privilege to have met her. I also met Coleen Townson Evans, who starred in some of Billy Graham's movies and authored several books, and her husband, Rev. Louis Evans Jr., also an author and well-known pastor.

There were some not-so-pleasant experiences. Once a mother who had just given birth began having a problem. I reported it to my superior who told me not to worry about it. But the lady continued to become more and more uncomfortable. I reported that also. Eventually the doctor arrived, saw the problem, and immediately started yelling "Why wasn't this taken care of?!" I got blamed for it and found it hard to hold back the tears.

The patient, a former nurse, comforted me after the others had left the room, saying, "Don't let it bother you. The nurse or student always gets blamed for things." But I didn't get chastised for it. My superiors at the School of Missionary Medicine believed me when I told them that I *did* report it.

Another time, the situation was just the opposite. I had the fun job of taking the newborn babies to their mothers. I picked up one of the babies, a girl, and noticed that she looked unusually blue. I uncovered her foot and flipped my finger against the bottom as I had been taught to do. She cried but still looked blue. So I took her to the supervising nurse instead of to her mother. This time I was praised. She did need some attention and was immediately cared for.

However, in spite of friends, interesting people, and interesting experiences, I missed my big football player. We wrote dozens of letters, but since I had finally decided to marry him, I didn't want to keep waiting. So I started trying to convince him to schedule the wedding during the Christmas break. He, being the practical type, felt we needed to save more money before the big event. But he did talk to his mother about it. She said, "You'd better marry her or you may lose her!"

Then he went to his pastor. Pastor Efaw said, "I think that's a great idea. You can work in California and go to school like you're doing now." So, Audy gave in, and we set the date for January 17, 1958. I would fly home as soon as the fall semester ended, and we could leave immediately after the wedding to return to California.

My good friends at SMM helped me with the planning and went with me to buy a wedding dress. Christine offered me her dress. She had looked so beautiful in it, but she was taller and more "curvaceous." There was no way of making it fit me. One of my friends said she knew of a place where I could get a nice dress for a reduced price and took me there along with my roommate.

We had lots of fun looking and trying on dresses. I finally found one I really liked. It didn't fit, but the sales lady told me it could be altered. The price, though, was $80, and I only had $50. At first she said they couldn't let me have it for fifty, but after checking with her boss, she finally said okay and that they would alter it for free. I had my beautiful dress, and my friends and I went back to the dorm walking on clouds. Wouldn't you like to buy a beautiful wedding dress today for $50?

In Huntington, Audy found friends were eager to help him too. One lady said she would make the cake. That would be her gift. What a gift! It was beautiful. Audy's family helped him send out the invitations, etc. I wanted Joyce Garrett to sing. She had such a beautiful voice and was like a second mother to me. She chose to do a duet with Mr. Van (John Van Pufflin) and play piano for him to do a solo. That was fine, as long as she participated, and Mr. and Mrs. Van had been special friends also.

I asked my sisters Christine and Priscilla to be my bridesmaids. My brother, Chad, who was now in the Air Force, could take leave and walk me down the aisle. By the time I arrived home, things were almost ready.

10

The Wedding, a Baby, and a Funeral

"Strengthened with all power, according to his glorious
might, for the attaining of all steadfastness and patience;
joyously…"

COLOSSIANS 1:11

The day of our wedding began with cold weather and a threat of
snow, but it didn't dampen our spirits. I was so grateful for all the
people who helped us with details. Instead of staying overnight in
Huntington, my family came up from Kentucky that morning to save
money. We had rehearsal in the early afternoon. Some friends came
down from Appalachian in addition to Mr. Van and Joyce Garrett.
Cookie King also came, which made me happy.

My sisters and I got dressed at the Roods' home, in-laws of Audy's
Aunt Chris. Her husband, Walter, drove us to the church. Everything
went smoothly, except that Chad got lost and was almost late. Chad
wore his dress Air Force uniform and gave me away. I don't think
I even invited Daddy to come. There had been almost no contact
with him for several years, and I don't think I even thought about it.

Pastor Efaw had to be away that weekend, so Pastor Stevens performed the ceremony. Audy's brother, Jennings, was his best man, and three friends, who had been so meaningful to him in his early Christian growth, joined him as groomsmen. Audy's sister Mary, then only seven, was the flower girl. Christine and Priscilla looked beautiful in the dresses Christine had made. Everything was done very simply, but full of meaning.

I was very excited and happy but also very nervous. I understand why some people want to get married at the Justice of the Peace office. I didn't really want to do that, but this was a big church and Audy's home church. I really didn't know how I was supposed to act. I had attended very few weddings and was afraid of doing something that would embarrass Audy. To display my affections so openly was something country folks never did, so that was hard for me too. I wanted to say my vows looking down at the floor! I didn't, and managed to get through it somehow.

As the recessional played, I took Audy's arm, and we started up the aisle with him leading at a fast pace. I almost tripped on the hem of my dress—it hadn't been shortened quite enough! I wore heels, but the aisle sloped upwards. I pulled on Audy's arm and whispered, "Slow down!" I picked up the front of my skirt and walked the rest of the way just fine.

We then went to the Efaw's home for the reception. Mrs. Efaw hadn't needed to go with her husband that weekend, and she organized everything. It was very crowded, but no one seemed to mind. I certainly enjoyed every minute of it, even getting some cake smashed in my face.

When the festivities ended, we said good-bye to family and friends and left for California. Audy traded vehicles with his brother, Jennings. We took his truck so that we could take all of our wedding presents as well as our other luggage and left Audy's car for him.

Audy's friends who had spent quite a bit of time tying old shoes, tin cans, etc. to Audy's car were very disappointed. And Jennings had to remove all that debris before going home that night!

It started snowing lightly. But we hadn't planned to go very far, just to a motel near the church where he had been the pastor. The couple Audy usually stayed with on Saturday nights had a son who owned a garage. He offered to give us some extra tires, in case we had any tire problems on our long trip to California. Unfortunately, we didn't make it that far. A tire decided to go flat before we reached the motel!

Audy maneuvered the truck off the road and stopped. There was no spare tire, and there was almost no traffic on the road at that time of night—about midnight. We had no choice but to sleep in the truck and get some help in the morning. All our wedding gifts were in the back of the truck, so Audy rummaged around until he found a couple of blankets. We wrapped ourselves up; he leaned against the door; I leaned against him, and we went to sleep. At least we were together! When we got cold, Audy would run the motor for a while, just to warm us up. And the snowflakes kept falling all through the night.

We were awakened by someone tapping on the window. It was a man driving a wrecker. "I was told there was somebody up here needing help," he announced. Praise the Lord! He fixed our tire. The roads were clear enough, and we drove on to Audy's friend's house, who fixed us a banquet of a breakfast. Their son gave us some tires, and we were on our way again. We stopped briefly to visit an uncle of mine and continued on until time to stop for the night—in a motel this time. Audy carried in our luggage while I checked us in.

I remember signing the register "Mr. and Mrs. Austin Lockhart." It was the first time I had written it and how thrilled I was to now be "Mrs. Austin Lockhart." I didn't mind being little when I had my big man with me.

Money was tight even though several people gave us money as wedding gifts. We ate pieces of the top layer of the wedding cake with purchased coffee for breakfast, snack things like cheese and crackers for lunch, and would have a good meal in a restaurant for dinner.

Going through some little western town, a policeman stopped us. Perhaps we were going too fast through their one-or-two-traffic-light borough, or it could have been the loud noise the truck was making. The muffler had developed a hole, which we couldn't afford to fix, so we were roaring along. The policeman didn't blow a whistle or anything, just waved both arms.

We stopped, and he opened the door on the passenger side. But of course, I was sitting close to Audy, and we kept our snack food against that door. The crackers, cheese, paper cups, and plates came rolling out onto the pavement. The policeman picked it up, put it back in the truck and with a wave of his arm, said disgustedly "Aaaa, just go on!" We laughed and laughed.

The last day was a long one, and Audy was getting pretty tired. I couldn't drive at that time even though Joyce had attempted to teach me, so he did all the driving. For a small town boy, arriving in Los Angeles was nerve-racking to say the least, with all those layered freeways. But we managed to weave our way through the maze and traffic and find the place I rented for us. It was only one room to ourselves—the bath, living room, and kitchen were all shared with others. But it was our first home, and it was very adequate for our needs. We arrived with a half tank of gas and only a few dollars. But I had a small check waiting for me at the school from working at the hospital. We could survive for a few more days.

There was not much time for rest as school was beginning soon. Audy found a job fairly quickly and started working and going to school at Biola. We became even closer friends with David and Vivian

Fox. It was so good to have friends from home. They helped us get acquainted with the area.

In just a few weeks, Audy also agreed to pastor a small church in a lovely picturesque setting called Carbon Canyon. The church provided a nice little cabin for us so that we could drive out on Fridays and spend the weekend. On Saturdays Audy would do some visiting in the community, while I studied. Sunday morning and evening he preached at the church. Afterward we would drive back to Los Angeles battling the heavy Sunday night traffic in time to get some sleep before beginning a new week. We were very busy, but very happy.

I marvel at how well Audy handled all of those things. He was only twenty-two. But I trusted him completely. I had struggled through a lot of things all by myself for a lot of years, and it was so wonderful to have this strong man—both physically and spiritually—to guide our lives. His dedication to God was remarkable, and we prayed about everything together. Audy was also knowledgeable in handling money—which I was not. He had worked since he was a small boy, starting with helping his uncle deliver papers, and he always had his own money. It was another area where I heaved a big sigh of relief and turned it all over to his more capable hands.

My role was to change in another way also. We had been married only a few months when I discovered I was pregnant. We had already decided that it would be wise to have a child before going to New Guinea. Since it was such a primitive place, and I had that episode in the hospital. We felt we needed to make sure there would be no unusual complications before we left our country of medical expertise. It was close enough to the end of school that I could finish and return home to Kentucky before the due date. We were very excited about the prospect of having our first child.

Vivian was already expecting, and it was fun going through this experience together.

Ralph Odman, the new General Director of the Unevangelized Fields Mission, was in California on other business and came to have the evening meal with us and to discuss our future. He suggested that Audy go to the Summer Institute of Linguistics as soon as the semester ended. "If you can tear yourselves apart," he added with a smile.

Since my course was a full twelve months, I wouldn't finish until almost the end of the summer. We knew it made sense, but it was very hard to carry out. Therefore, after only a few months of marriage, my husband kissed me good-bye, and left for Norman, Oklahoma. I admit to shedding a few tears.

About three months later, I graduated. I took and passed the California state board exams, getting my Licensed Practical Nurse degree. I was *finally* totally finished with school. I had been in some kind of educational program almost continuously since I was four years old—twenty years! However, when I thought about it, I was so grateful to God that I had received all that training while I was free to do so. After children come, it is hard to fit schooling into a busy schedule.

I worked a few weeks in the mail room at Biola and then flew home to my mother's. Audy came as soon as he finished his course, and we stayed at my mother's until our little girl arrived.

Audy did have to leave me again for a few days to attend the Missions Conference at Grace Gospel Church in Huntington. I was expecting to deliver any time, so I couldn't go. No matter, the good folks at Grace gave us a baby shower anyway. Audy had a wonderful time presenting for the first time what we believed God wanted us to do. He did make it back in time for the arrival of our first child.

I decided to have my baby at my mother's home rather than going to a hospital. My pregnancy had been absolutely normal, and I would have both a midwife and a doctor with me. My sister Ivallean was away getting her Master's Degree in nursing. But Evelyn Mottrom, her partner in her years as a midwife in Kentucky, still worked in Hindman with Dr. Barker, my doctor since coming back from California.

When the time came, I sent Audy with a note describing my symptoms to Evelyn, who came right away. Dr. Barker came a bit later. And very shortly thereafter, Leah Ellen Lockhart made her presence in this world known by loud wailing!

I thought she was the most beautiful baby I had ever seen. She was absolutely perfect, and I had no complications. We were so thankful to God. A few weeks later our friend Jack Keeney, who had been Audy's young people's director, came to Mom's house, bringing all the items from the Baby Shower—heaps of things, everything needed and more. (All four of my daughters used many of the items.)

Very soon after Leah's birth, we began visiting churches. I was acquainted with several pastors in the area because of my association with Camp Nathanael. We presented the needs of the Dutch New Guinea people and told of our burden to take the gospel to them. Many of the churches wanted to support us but had little money. Some pledged only ten dollars per month. But we were grateful for it and felt very honored because, for many, we were their first missionaries.

❖ ❖ ❖

After visiting many churches in Kentucky, we felt it was time to move to Huntington. It had been great being there with Mom and Priscilla. I hated to go, and I know it was hard for them to let us take baby Leah away, but we needed to raise the rest of our support. Friends from Grace Church had an empty apartment which they offered to let us use, though they were trying to rent it, and occasionally would bring someone in to look at it. That was only a minor inconvenience, and we appreciated their generosity.

We visited a lot of churches and eventually raised enough support for the mission to say we could plan our departure for June, 1959. Grace even held a good-bye dinner for us which Austin's mother, Pauline, attended with us. Pastor Stevens had led her to faith in Christ only a few weeks earlier. So this was a great occasion, as we celebrated her new birth as well as our coming departure.

We continued our speaking engagements. When we returned from one of them and went to visit Pauline, we found she had just gotten out of the hospital following gall bladder surgery. She said her doctor told her that she had the heart of an old woman, although she was only forty-eight. We were concerned but didn't realize the severity of it.

Just a few weeks later, we were enjoying a meal with a couple from the church, when a call came for Audy. His mother had suffered a heart attack and died almost instantly. I can't describe the shock and the pain it was for me, and I knew that for Audy the pain was many times more than what I felt. It was so sudden and so devastating.

We hastily said good-bye to our hosts and went to his mother's home. She had already been taken to the funeral home. The children gave us more details. Audy's father, Olen, an alcoholic, had only been out of jail a few days. Some of his drinking buddies came by, and Olen left with them. It was then that Pauline had her heart attack. That added to the pain and turmoil that many were feeling. There were still five children at home. Sam was about sixteen, Linda about eleven, Mary, eight, and the twins, Gary and Terry, only five. What would become of the children was already storming the minds of everyone.

The house started filling up with people. Pastor and Mrs. Efaw came, and neighbors, and relatives. Some of us noticed that Gary and Terry were sitting at the table because they hadn't had supper! Some ladies and I began cooking, and fed anyone who was hungry. How tragic it was for the children. Olen heard the news and came back, but he was not capable of handling even the present situation, much less taking care of the children in the future.

Audy's older brother, Jennings, and wife Barbara came up from Florida as soon as they could get there. Glen, the brother just younger than Audy, was newly married. He and Norma arrived. Audy and I moved into his mother's home so that we could help take care of the young children. All the children together with Olen planned the funeral.

Many relatives I had not met before came. But Chris and Walter Rood were traveling back from vacationing in Florida, and many tried in vain to reach them (no cell phones in those days). Chris learned of her sister's death when she reached home and a neighbor asked her if she had just returned from the funeral. "What funeral?" she asked, and the neighbor reluctantly told her. Such a sad time! But those who knew the Lord took comfort in knowing Pauline had accepted the Savior and was now with Him.

After the funeral, the big question on everyone's mind was, "What is the best way to care for the children?" Audy and I offered to cancel our plans of going overseas and to help take care of them in whatever way we could, though in our hearts we wondered why God brought us this far if we were now to stay home. Maybe so we would still carry the burden for New Guinea and encourage others to go? We didn't know. But we felt it our duty to help the family. We also offered to adopt some of the children and take them with us to New Guinea or stay home with them, whatever the family felt was best.

Jennings, however, felt very strongly that all the children should be kept in one household, and that he, as the oldest child, should be the one to keep them. We should go ahead with our plans. He and Barb also felt that it would be best for them to live on a farm where there would be plenty of room.

So the search began for a place. Audy, Leah, and I moved to a room in Pastor Stevens' house so that Jennings and Barb could move in with the children and begin their lives as the new parents of eight children (three of their own, and Jennings' five siblings). They later had another child, bringing the grand total to nine! They eventually found a farm in a rural area north of Charleston, West Virginia. Audy did as much as he could to help them get settled.

Then we resumed our preparations to go to New Guinea. We had cancelled our first booking. Another couple from another mission was able to take our places on the ship. UFM was able to get us a new booking for September, leaving from Long Beach, California. We left Huntington, West Virginia, August 17, 1959.

11

New Guinea at Last

"We persuade men . . . for the love of Christ controls us."

2 Corinthians 5:11, 14

Austin traded in his car for an old but functional truck. Men from Grace Gospel helped pack and load everything onto the truck. Mom and Priscilla and Chris and Don, with little Loren Dale, came to see us off. We said our tearful good-byes and set out for California once again. It had been three months since our first departure date and almost two years since our first trip to California, our honeymoon trip.

This time we had baby Leah against the passenger's side door. Friends bought us a travel bed, which fit perfectly in that spot. We had already traveled so many miles presenting the needs of New Guinea to many churches that Leah was used to the travel and did very well. We were happy and excited to finally be going but sad as well. My Mom could have used my help, and Audy's family needed him. But we felt this was what God wanted us to do.

First we went to Michigan, Joyce Garrett's home state. She had introduced us to several pastors whose churches supported her. Audy presented the needs of New Guinea to those churches, and two of them contributed to our work for several years.

I also wanted to visit my father. It had been about five years since I had seen him. I didn't want to go to his home, so he met us at our hotel, and we had a good visit. He was happy to meet my new husband and his first granddaughter. From that time on, Daddy wrote to us fairly often, and we were able to rekindle a father-daughter and grandpa relationship.

We then traveled South and West toward California. We decided to cross the desert at night when it wouldn't be so hot. While we waited, we slept a few hours on the truck. A mattress was on the very top of a lot of boxes, drums, and crates. We felt it would be comfortable enough for a short nap. I climbed up first. Audy handed Leah to me, and he followed. We put Leah between us, keeping her safe, and slept very comfortably. Audy then drove all night and until the sun began getting hot. We found a motel then, and slept in the cool air conditioning. The next day we were past the desert area.

Our time in California with David and Vivian Fox was great. Leah found a playmate in their daughter, and the two little girls entertained us. In a few days we boarded the ship in Long Beach, California. Neither of us had even seen a ship that big, and we were taking a three-week trip on this one.

I found the trip to be a mixture of pleasure and stress. Pleasure in seeing interesting places, meeting friendly people, and eating delicious food. However, it was stressful trying to keep up with our nine-month-old little girl. We had to make sure our cabin door was always closed. If it wasn't, she would get out and start climbing the stairs to the next deck. When we went up to any of the public decks, we could not put her down on the floor. It was not safe. We were thankful that we didn't have severe sea sickness, but the constant mild nausea was not pleasant. Nevertheless, overall it was an experience of a lifetime.

The ship docked in Honolulu, then Fiji, before arriving in Auckland, New Zealand. It was on a Sunday and the ship would be in Auckland all day, so we decided to look for a church. Finding one nearby, we entered and immediately saw that this was a gem. The people were very friendly, and the message was good.

After the service we learned that the church supported some missionaries with the Australian branch of our mission. We also learned that whenever a ship was in the harbor, volunteers were prepared to invite any visitors to their home for dinner. We happily accepted the invitation and had a wonderful visit with our hosts and enjoyed a good meal. Following lunch they took us sightseeing around the island.

About mid-afternoon, our hostess asked me, "How are you for nappies?" I had no idea what she meant and it probably showed on my face. "Oh," she said, "I think you call them diapers." Both of us laughed. We both spoke English, but there were quite a few differences. I assured her I had enough. Our new friends drove us back to the ship after a lovely, interesting day. How wonderful to find fellow Christians and feel such a connection, though we had never met before.

The remainder of the trip across the ocean and our flight from Australia to New Guinea is all covered in *A Missionary's Journal* by Austin Lockhart. We were so happy to be on our way. We had been praying, talking, and planning about going to New Guinea for several years, and it was now becoming a reality.

We arrived in Sentani, Dutch New Guinea, in October of 1959. The journey took more than two months, and we traveled almost halfway around the world. Who would have thought that this little girl from Hollybush, from a broken home, and this football player with an alcoholic father, and now without a mother, would be chosen by God to help with this ministry! We were bringing the gospel to the primitive, cannibalistic tribal people of New Guinea. We didn't realize at the time what a historic endeavor this was. Still, we were almost overcome with gratitude for the honor God entrusted to us, yet fearful that we would fall short of doing what God wanted us to do.

Ralph and Melba Maynard met us at the airport. I had known them since my college days at Bryan. They were with me in language school and in candidate school. I was glad to be able to introduce them to my husband and child. Ralph was now going to be our field leader. He was a great leader, and we remained friends for many years, long after our missionary service was over.

We met many other missionaries in Sentani from an assortment of missions.

- MAF (Missionary Aviation Fellowship). They were the ones to fly us interior and bring us supplies and mail.
- RBMU (Regions Beyond Missionary Union).
- CAMA (Christian and Missionary Alliance).
- The Australian Branch of UFM, which later became APCM (Asia and Pacific Christian Mission).
- TEAM (The Evangelical Alliance Mission).
- It was a wonderful group of men and women, all in New Guinea for the same purpose—to tell the tribal people that there is a God who loves them and that Jesus died for them. Until the coming of the missionary, most of these people lived their lives for generations with little contact with the outside world.

We stayed about a week on the coast and were then flown to the interior, to Mulia, American UFM's only station. Australian UFM had two stations—Bokondini and Kelila. John Greenfield, an American, and New Zealander, Meno Heyblom, were also attempting to establish a work in a different tribe on the far side of DNG near the Papua New Guinea border.

Our flight into Mulia was our time was our first time riding in a small, four-seat Cessna 180 airplane. Paul Pontier ("Pablo") was our pilot. We took only the bare necessities since Pablo told us we could take a total of only 580 pounds. Audy weighed about 200 lbs. Leah and I together added about 135 lbs. That didn't leave us many pounds to spare. As we took off, both Audy and I were a bit apprehensive, though we trusted in our pilot's skills and in God's protection.

How special it was seeing the lush mountains and valleys from the air! The small Cessna airplanes fly at a much lower altitude than the big jets, and you can see everything clearly. It was all beautiful. The landing at Mulia was rough, but thankfully, short. He taxied up near the houses and turned off the motor.

As soon as the propeller stopped turning, Rie Dedecker came over and opened the door. Leah reached for her, and they were friends instantly. Ralph had returned a few days ahead of us, though Mel remained on the coast recovering from an episode of amoebic dysentery. He introduced us to the others: Dave and Dina Cole, from Canada, with Larry in the stroller, and Rie, a nurse from Holland. Another American couple, Leon and Loraine Dillinger, were temporarily helping at Kelela, one of APCM's stations. Cole's son, Larry, and Maynard's son, Tim, were both about Leah's age. I was glad Leah would have playmates.

Nationals swarmed around us, asking questions, mostly about Leah. They were all black-skinned, and she was the first white girl child they had seen. They were fascinated with her curly blond hair and kept stroking her head and biting on their bent forefingers, a sign of amazement! Fortunately Leah didn't seem afraid.

They were a friendly lot, but how strange they looked! Wearing almost no clothing, dirty, many were painted with a black greasy something. Many had great masses of hair, covered with coarse, loosely woven nets, some had hair cut short. The women wore string skirts, with large net bags draped over their backs and a band across the top of the head. We, of course, had seen pictures, but it's much different when seeing them in person. We kept smiling and speaking our greetings in English.

Ralph led the way to the building which was to be our home for the next year. It was the far half of a duplex, with Ralph and Mel living in the other half. We took a quick look around. It was much nicer than I expected. Dina and Rie had supplied most of our needs. Two cots were in the bedroom; a clumsy wooden box, its sides made of green plastic screen, stood in the living room—Leah's bed. There was also a shower area and a kitchen with a cast iron, wood-burning stove and a counter built of split bark and round poles.

We were called for coffee and cookies at Cole's place—a similar looking building, with Rie living in the other half of the duplex. We were told later that the Dani people thought Rie was also Dave's wife. But they straightened it out eventually. After coffee, we were invited to also have the noon meal with them. Good! I wouldn't have to start coping with primitive life just yet.

Mulia was a wide, long valley with lush, green vegetation surrounded by huge mountains. All the houses had a breathtaking "down-valley" view. Up valley too was gorgeous, having a smaller mountain farther away with majestic rocks jutting out here and there. The weather was clear blue skies with warm sunshine on most days and rains coming in the late afternoon almost every day.

The missionaries already had lots of colorful flowers growing along rock-lined paths and in the yards. We were walking on clouds. It was so good to be here at last. Everything and everyone was so nice! But we knew we had lots to learn.

We settled into our new home with borrowed beds, pots and pans, towels—I even borrowed some of Mel's dresses. We didn't mind at first, thinking it would be only a short while until our own things, which we had shipped from California, arrived. Not so! Weeks went by before our crates and drums arrived on the coast, and more weeks before being released from customs. After that, MAF was busy and couldn't give us many flights, so things came slowly.

We needed (I *wanted*) our dishes badly. We requested that drum number two, which contained them, be brought in on the next flight. When the plane arrived, Dave Steiger hopped out, flashed his broad smile and drawled, "I hope I've brought the right drum. I thought you asked for drum number two, but my wife thought it was number one, so I brought number one." Tools! We would have to wait some more for our dishes. I decided I might as well get used to the slow pace of most things in that country.

When our drums finally arrived, I set about trying to make our little duplex a bit more "homey." I hung curtains, covered cushions, and arranged things as attractively as possible. The mattress, which friends had given us, made a comfortable bed. Audy built us some living room furniture with round poles and bark. With cushions added, it was really quite comfortable. Built-in shelves sufficed for dressers and for cupboards in the kitchen.

When I started cooking, I found that a wood stove wasn't very different from the coal stove my Mom cooked on while I was growing up. You only had to remember to feed it more often. Other things, however, were much more taxing, like the aluminum kitchen roof.

The panels had been used previously. Consequently, there were lots of nail holes, plugged rather ineffectively with tiny sticks wrapped with bits of cloth. Not wanting to add more nail holes so that they could be used again, the panels were held in place with large rocks. When it rained, depending on the direction of the wind, Audy had to stand on a chair and rearrange the roof. The rest of the house had a thatched roof.

My first experience with a houseboy occurred just a few days after arriving at Mulia. We had just finished breakfast, when a young Dani boy came to my door with a note from Dina Cole. The note read, "This boy could work for you, do your dishes and such." I looked at him. He was about eleven or twelve years old, smiling from ear to ear, but his body was very dirty, and he was totally naked, as was the custom.

What should I do? I didn't know a word of his language, and he didn't know a word of mine. I decided to plunge in. So, talking in English, and using a lot of pantomime, I got him started doing the dishes with two pans of water—one soapy, one for rinsing, and towels on the side for draining. When I handed him a tea towel for drying the dishes, he threw it over his dirty shoulder. After a while it slid off and landed on the floor. Before I could get to the towel to retrieve it, he picked it up—with his toes! This would never do!

About that time Dina called from her porch, "Did he take a bath?" "No," I answered. "Send him down to the river to bathe," she said. I did know where the river was, so I pointed in that direction, using more English words, and thankfully, he went. He returned a bit cleaner, and Dina brought down some clothes for him. He finally finished the dishes, though I washed them over again as soon as he was gone.

A few days later, I noticed the bottle brush that I used for washing Leah's bottles, had small black hairs tangled in the bristles. When I asked him about it (as best I could) he "innocently" stated that his head had itched, so he scratched it—with the bottle brush!

Things improved as I learned more of the language. I tried several houseboys though, before finding a young boy named Aletit. He was great—clean, willing to work, and eager to learn. He even learned some English just by listening to Audy and me talking to each other. Then he wrote it down in his own phonetic system. He worked for us until we left Mulia.

Only one day after our arrival, Ralph told us there was to be a pig feast in a nearby village. "Just down the hill and across the creek. We should all go down for a while," he said. We were delighted. Imagine getting to go to a pig feast so soon. About ten o'clock some men came to tell us that all was ready. We donned hats to protect us from the sun and followed the messengers.

As we descended the embankment, I noticed something that made my heart skip a beat. Down by the stream were dozens of native folks holding large rocks. Now I had not yet learned that these people were not the least bit hostile. I had heard a great deal before leaving home about the dangers we would face. So my thinking went something like this: What are they going to do with so many rocks? What if they decide they don't like us and start throwing the rocks at us?

I glanced at Dina, who was nearest to me, then at the others. No one seemed the least bit concerned. I *casually* asked, "What are the rocks for?"

"Oh," Dina answered, "they're for cooking the food. They build a huge fire and put the rocks on top until they're hot. Then they pack them with the food in leaf-lined pits—works like an oven." I relaxed.

We were at the stream. The people smiled shyly at us as we passed them. We climbed to the plateau. Those with the rocks followed, and we watched as they placed the rocks on top of piles of wood, arranged in a long neat bed. When the rocks had all been arranged, they set the wood on fire.

A huge crowd already gathered. Men sat in one group and women and children in another. We sat in between. All awaited the killing of the pigs, which I would just as soon have skipped. When it was over, lots of people began milling about. The pits had already been dug, about three feet wide and two feet deep. Lined with banana leaves and ferns, they were ready for sweet potatoes, greens, and the pig, as soon as it was butchered (with bamboo knives which were amazingly sharp). Hot rocks were alternated with the food and more leaves. A little water was added with each layer. The women placed all the food, and the men placed the hot rocks. It was fascinating watching how they all worked together with such efficiency. On the very top, more banana leaves, dirt and more rocks were packed tightly.

We went home for a while. About two hours later, we were called to come and participate in the feast. They were very polite in serving, treating us as honored guests. We enjoyed watching every detail, if not every bite of food. Some of the meat had too much fat for our liking. Ralph explained to us that the fat is considered the best part. Giving it to us was a part of honoring us. Later Ralph asked the men if it was alright for us to take some home so we wouldn't have to eat it, and they seemed happy for us to do that.

❖ ❖ ❖

My letters to my family during these first weeks were mostly about family, especially about Leah getting her first teeth, learning to talk, etc., and "Leah has started 'praying' with us now. When we bow our heads, she bows hers also and puts her hands over her eyes, (usually peeking between her fingers) and mumbles." But a letter to my sister Ivallean also contained the following:

This morning Audy and I went with the nurse (Rie
Dedecker) up to a little village to see her houseboy's
father who was sick. They were having a pig feast
(much smaller than the other one), sacrificing pigs to the
evil spirits, trying to get rid of the sickness. However,
they know that Rie has helped many others, so they
welcomed us, and we crawled inside the native hut. All
the chiefs of nearby villages were there, so it was quite
crowded. Rie went over and examined the patient and
"gave him a needle," (the way they express it.) They
wanted us to stay and help them eat the pig, but Rie
told them my baby might be crying (we had left her
with Dina), and we needed to go. It was the first time I
had been inside a native hut. It would be high enough
to stand up in, but they make two levels, the top for
sleeping, and the lower part for cooking, with the fire
in a small clay-lined pit in the middle of the room.
Everything is all black with smoke.

We were very busy right away getting settled and studying the
Dani language, though not much of the language was written at that
time. Austin helped work on the new home Ralph and Mel were
building and on expanding the air strip. He usually worked with Dave
Cole who taught him the details of constructing a good functional
strip, knowledge which he needed in the next few years.

It was very important that the airstrip slope so that the rain could
quickly drain away. It needed to be as smooth as possible for the
safety of the airplane and pilot, with no sharp rocks that could slit a
tire and no ridges that could make the plane bounce too much. And

no animals on the strip! Every time a plane was due, someone had to walk the full length of the strip, making sure everything was safe.

One morning when a plane was due, and Dave Cole was doing the inspection, suddenly a large pig ran onto the strip. Dave tried to chase him off, with no luck, and the plane was only a few minutes away. Dave ran to the house to get Ralph's gun, which was kept in Maynard's bedroom. They were away, and in his panic, Dave forgot that a single lady was visiting and sleeping in that bedroom. He dashed in to get the gun, waking the lady, who apparently was so surprised that she just stared at him. He found the gun, ran out again, and took care of the pig before the plane arrived.

Later when Dave recounted the story to a group of missionaries, someone asked Dave what he said to the lady. Before he could answer, my husband exclaimed, "He said, 'Have Gun, Will Travel!'" It was the perfect retort and brought many laughs whenever the story was told. For those who may not remember, "Have Gun, Will Travel" was the title of a very popular TV show many years ago.

❖ ❖ ❖

Plans were being made to open a new station a day-and-a-half walk from Mulia. Audy and Dave Cole would be the ones to go to build the airstrip. For a while it was planned that we and Coles would move there when the airstrip was finished.

However as our first Christmas on the field was approaching Audy, who was the picture of health, began having serious stomach pains. Rie checked him out and concluded that he had appendicitis. Reluctantly, he decided to go to the coast for surgery if necessary. It turned out to be necessary, and Leah and I had our Christmas without him. We did have a good Christmas dinner with Maynards. The Coles were at the coast also, and Rie was visiting friends. Audy returned home the day before New Year's.

As soon as he was able, Austin and Dave Cole started building up their strength by doing a series of treks around Mulia. And in March 1960, they left for the big trek.

A letter to my mother reads:

Audy and Dave left yesterday for Ilu. One young man, who went halfway with them, came back this afternoon. He said they were getting along okay, and that they got plenty of carriers to go the rest of the way with them. In another day or two, a carrier will probably come bringing us a note from them. They have a radio on which they can hear us talk to them but have no way of talking to us. Friday, the plane is going to drop some more food and supplies to them. They expect to be gone almost two months—seems an awfully long time, but then we are eager to have the place ready for us to move up there.

A letter to my sister:

Audy was home for a week. Everyone said he looked like Castro with his long beard. He shaved it off, but it has probably grown back by now.

This past month and a half has been pretty hectic for all of us here at Mulia. Believe it or not, we have had only a few days here and there when we haven't had company! At first two men came for a committee meeting, staying a week; another man who had been sick [John Greenfield, who helped us later] came for a rest and stayed about two weeks. A lady came before he left, staying a week.

Then a man from Africa on his way home for furlough stopped by for a few weeks. He doesn't plan to go back to Africa and is interested in coming to DNG [This was Ray Holley, who later helped us at Kiwi]. Then a Doctor from the Rockefeller Institute of Medical Research came to do research on the goiters at Mulia [many of the women had huge goiters on their necks]. He stayed three days. When he left a new couple arrived, and while they will be here permanently, they are company while they're new. Whew! I'm glad it's not this way all the time.

A letter came by carrier from Austin:

Just a quick note to let you know that I arrived back from Mulia okay. I arrived about 9:30 Sunday morning. Good time for a beginner, huh? Good trip except for a ledge above one of the mountain streams that fell out from under me early the last morning. I'm thankful that I hardly got a scratch from the fall. I got dunked in the water and my camera got wet (the camera wasn't ruined), but all else was okay except for a few sore muscles.

At last the Ilu strip was finished, and Austin was home again. My husband tells this story in *A Missionary's Journal*.

It was time for our first field conference, which was held on the Bokondini station combined with the Austrailian part of UFM. Then three momentous things happened—one before conference, one during, and one after.

12

Transition

> "I have been crucified with Christ; and it is no longer I
> who live, but Christ who lives in me."
>
> GALATIANS 2: 20A

We looked forward to Conference and the opportunity to get acquainted with our Australian and New Zealander counterparts. It proved to be even more enjoyable than expected. Our use of the English language may have been different, but we found them very likable and certainly just as dedicated to the cause of reaching the New Guinea people with the gospel as we were. Bokondini was about twice as wide as the Mulia valley, with large grassy areas between the houses as well as the usual high mountains. Beautiful!

One day Ralph asked us to wait for him. He had something to discuss with us as we walked up to our rooms. I could hardly believe my ears when he asked, "How would you folks feel about going to Sibil?"

"Well," Audy answered after some hesitation, "I must admit it is an entirely new idea to us," he said, looking at me. "But we would have no real objections." I agreed.

"It's not definite at all," Ralph added, "Both you and the Sadliers are being considered. I just wanted to know how you felt about it."

"You folks decide," Audy said. "We are willing either way."

He left us then, and Audy and I just looked at each other. "Imagine, Sibil!" The Sibil valley is in the Star Mountains where John Greenfield and Menno Heyblom had been working. It was very near to the Papua New Guinea border. We had heard discussions about the need there since John Greenfield had become ill. The more we thought about it, the more we liked the idea, though I knew that I would be the only white woman in that area.

The next day Ralph told us we had been chosen. Stan and Barb Sadlier would go to Ilu. That was the second momentous thing to happen to us.

The first one occurred before conference and was one of the hardest things we had ever faced. Leah became so ill that we didn't think she would live through the night. God was with us, however, and showed us that He could take care of us in any circumstance, anywhere He put us. Praise God, Leah recovered. The story is in *A Missionary's Journal*. On this new assignment we would be completely without medical help for most of the time, and we needed that assurance from God.

In July 1960, sandwiched between field conference and moving to Sibil, the third momentous thing occurred. Another daughter, Elizabeth (Beth), entered the world, our family, and our hearts.

Letters to my family after arriving at Sibil read:

We arrived at our new home a week ago and are partially settled. Everything is very different. The weather is much warmer, like the coastal areas. We have a lot more bugs, and I'm happy that we brought a screened-in crib for

Leah. When I put her to bed at night, I can just close the lid, and she is safe from all the mosquitoes, spiders, etc. Since Beth is still a baby, I can cover her basket with netting. The house, top and sides, is built with aluminum panels. The kitchen and living room floors are concrete, but the bedrooms are gravel. Yes gravel! At least I don't have to do much sweeping—just rake the gravel once in a while to level it out! Two inside walls are of woven bamboo, like the ones at Mulia, the others are aluminum. Audy made me a couch, and I covered it with blue material. The curtains have blue flowers, so it looks quite pretty.

These people had never seen white children before, so we have spectators all day long, especially when I give Beth a bath or feed her with a bottle. We keep her by the window in the living room in a large basket made for us by another missionary. It is shaped like a bassinet with plaited vine trimming on the top— really pretty. I padded and lined it, and with a mattress made to fit, it is quite comfortable, I'm sure.

Leah's hair (very blonde) is also quite fascinating to the people. They can't seem to say the 'th' in Beth's name. It comes out 'Bes' or 'Beso.' They put an 'o' on the end of a lot of words. Leah is 'Yela.' They pronounce an 'l' as a 'y' at the beginning of a word. They have no vowels together, so insert an 'l' between the 'e' and 'a.' We have made a big sand box out back for Leah, and she spends a lot of time out there. People come along and with great patience teach her how to say many of their words. Maybe I should go out and play with her so I can learn faster!

> My medical work here consists mostly of giving penicillin
> shots for yaws and treatment for malaria, both very
> rampant. There aren't as many burns since they usually
> don't need heat in their houses.

Our house was only a few yards from a small lake. It looked beautiful, though we didn't use the water because it was too stagnant. Fresh rain water was better. Of course I didn't have disposable diapers in those days, so diapers had to be washed. I tried to teach my house help to rinse the diapers in the lake. However, I soon noticed that my supply of diapers was dwindling. Finally I discovered the houseboys had been putting the diapers on the end of a stick and swishing them back and forth in the water. Many dropped off the stick and got lost in the lake. We quickly found other ways to rinse the diapers!

❖ ❖ ❖

We had very few airplanes coming in, but since we were on a government station we could sometimes send mail out on government planes.

In a letter to my sister Ivy dated October 28, 1960, I wrote: "I just heard that a government plane is coming on Monday (This is Friday). I want to get all my letters answered since we won't have an MAF flight until the last of November." After thanking her for some clothing she had sent for Leah and Beth, I added "I've put away the sleeping bags for a colder climate. We expect to move again in about a year to another mountainous area which will be colder."

We didn't have fresh vegetables at Sibil like we did at Mulia. I did the best I could with what was available. I must have done okay. Audy wrote this to my Mom:

"Lorrie is becoming the queen of conglomerations. She really does a good job of making a variety of good dishes out of cans."

Sometimes I got things from home and could make something nice.

To my sister again:

I've been baking fruitcakes today—took me about half an hour to de-bug and de-worm the fruit and flour before I could mix the dough, so all together it has been a long process. . . though well worth it!

Between here and the Baliem valley (Dani area) there are thousands of people who have not been reached. As we flew over, we saw some villages having as many as 70 houses (most Dani villages don't have more than 10)—and naturally we long to reach them. Many of them probably speak different languages, and it would take many days of trekking to get there. The area we are considering is in that direction but speaks the same language as here, though a different dialect. As soon as another couple or two come out to help us, we want to open a station there. Then in years to come, perhaps the other areas can be reached from that point. We sure need lots of people to help in the work here.

This was the vision of the field council. I wrote my letter October 28, 1960. I marvel that this is exactly what happened. It was God's vision planted in the hearts of those He had called to accomplish it.

❖ ❖ ❖

The language at Sibil was a new one for us. We had not become fluent in the Dani language but were beginning to feel more comfortable with it. It was hard to start all over again. We were grateful for the help of Menno Heyblom and spent as much time as possible in language study. But since Menno was with the Australian branch of UFM (APCM), he was soon moved to Kelilia and we were on our own.

Sibil didn't prove to be very strategic for reaching the most people, and only a few months after our arrival, it was decided that it would be better to speed up the opening of a place called Kiwirok. The area had already been surveyed from the air and a suitable site for an airstrip selected. Plans had been made to place the next available couple there. Therefore, after some urging from Austin, the field council approved plans for us to move to "Kiwi" as soon as possible.

On December 8, 1960, missionaries and carriers from the Dani area arrived to help Audy, and they brought supplies with them. We spent the remainder of that day collecting other needed items and finding more carriers. I helped with preparing and packing food for the journey. I was apprehensive about their going into unknown territory. Would they be safe? Would the people be friendly? Yet I was excited about reaching more people—those "back rows"—with the gospel.

The next morning the men left for the long strenuous trek to the Kiwi Valley. (Told in detail in *A Missionary's Journal*.)

We were already expecting Bob Johanson, a pilot, and his wife, Carol, along with their son, David, who was Leah's age, to come for a few days of vacation. They arrived on the tenth. Bob planned to drop more supplies to the men after they arrived on the Kiwi plateau. Whenever a large drop was scheduled, someone, usually a man, would go along to push things out the door of the airplane as the pilot swooped down over the area and tilted the plane.

Since no man was available, and Carol was pregnant, I was supposed to go. It wasn't really dangerous, the pusher was always strapped in, but I was a bit nervous anyway. However, Bob was more comfortable having Carol do it in spite of her pregnancy. The two of them made several drops of digging instruments, burlap bags (for carrying away the dirt), and more food. We baked dozens of cookies and spent a lot of time taking peanut butter out of glass jars and putting it into metal cans which would be safe for dropping.

Leah enjoyed having a playmate. She had missed Tim Maynard and Larry Cole, her friends at Mulia. But she and David bonded quickly and had fun together.

Bob and Carol stayed with me until after Christmas. I was alone for a few days. Then Mel Maynard and Tim came and stayed until the Kiwi air strip was finished. Tim and Leah enjoyed playing together, and Mel and I enjoyed talking. One day we suddenly realized that Leah and Tim had been unusually quiet for a while. When we found them, they were happily spreading margarine all over that concrete kitchen floor. There was no getting it clean again—ever!

John Greenfield came a little later. He had lived at Sibil for about two years (with Menno Heyblom) but had some serious medical problems. At first, it was thought to be a nervous breakdown, but later he received the correct diagnosis of porphyria, a rare blood disease with multiple disorders. Audy and I hoped he would be well enough to help us once we got to Kiwi, especially with the language. His job at Sibil would be to help get things ready for loading the planes, which would move us to Kiwi, and to help with the loading when moving day arrived.

Dave Cole couldn't wait for the airstrip to be finished. Dina was expecting the arrival of their second child soon, and he needed to get home. This child, another boy, arrived healthy. They named him, Bruce. So he walked out, leaving the Kiwi plateau on December 26. The following is part of the letter Dave brought to me form Audy:

It's the night before Christmas as I begin to write. Since Dave is leaving day after tomorrow, Ralph, Leon, and I are all sitting around the table writing to our wives and listening to Christmas music. It doesn't seem much like Christmas, but I guess that's understandable. Ralph made a frame, shaped something like a Christmas tree and hung it over the table. He put strings of the decorations you sent to us on it and hung a big red balloon at the bottom. We have plenty food, even snack food—peanuts, cookies, etc. We'll have the two chickens for our dinner tomorrow. Ralph is doing a good job with the cooking, so we are getting along fine in that area.

I'm spending most of my time on the strip, and Leon is working on the house. My plan is that Leon build a small building first—two bedrooms and a kitchen—then start the frame for an aluminum roofed house, like the plan I drew up some time ago. It will take a lot longer to finish. We can live in the small one in the beginning.

I find I'm missing you more and more. I'm so very thankful for you. I'm realizing more and more how much I love you. It's so good to have a wife and children to come home to. I'm glad for you that you have the children to keep you company when I'm away like this. Give Leah and Beth big kisses from me, and tell them Daddy hopes to be home soon. May God be your sufficiency in my absence.

There followed a full page of instructions mostly for John on the order of sending things over to Kiwi, removing some things from the Sibil house and closing it up.

Then this P. S.: "May the coming New Year bring much blessing. Next time send a long, long, long letter. I like to spend my evenings in thought over them."

We moved to Kiwi January 31, 1961.

On the Plateau

"Home is where the heart is."

"God has a purpose for each one of us, a work for each
one to do, an influence for each one to exert, a likeness
to His dear son to manifest, and then a place for each
one to fill in His holy temple."

ARTHUR C. A. HALL

Approaching the Kiwi airstrip for the first time, I felt much like I
do when driving on a major highway with large trucks on either side
of me. The airstrip consumed the major portion of the plateau, which
was hemmed in by large high mountains on both sides. I was glad
our pilot, Bob Johanson, had already made one successful landing
that morning and was very skilled in manipulating his aircraft. We
landed safely.

On the ground I could see that there was enough room on the
left side of the plateau for several buildings. A temporary, three-room
"hut" had already been erected which would be our home for the

next few months, until a larger more permanent home could be built. Just beyond that area, the plateau dropped off about eighty feet, straight down to the river below. The river curved in such a way that it also cut off the plateau at the bottom end of the airstrip, necessitating the strip to be only 1300 feet, just barely meeting MAF's requirements.

Our first letter from the Kiwirok plateau, written by Austin to our friends and family in America:

"Ne kato," "I don't know" is the answer we received from the people of the Kiwirok valley, when asked if they knew anything about God. We trust that this answer will soon be changed. As of February 1, we have established a mission station in the valley. We have been trying to teach them the truths of the Gospel, and we are pleased that they seem to be eager to hear.

The people can't get over the fact that one family has "so many things." Even though in our thinking, we have only the bare necessities of life; to them we are rich. They are always looking with admiration at the buttons on our clothes, especially the white ones, and asking us to rip them off so they can wear them on their noses. Then, there are the chickens; the men can't understand our letting them live just to get the eggs, when the feathers would make such nice headpieces! Almost every time a stranger comes by, he wants to see my possessions— wife, children, house, etc. They never cease to be amazed by them.

These people are different from the Dani people. Their features are more Indian-like. They are very colorful with

their red paint, slender long drums, and artistically carved
arrows, though they don't have the long spears.

❖ ❖ ❖

We had indeed "arrived." From the first day, we felt that this was
where we belonged. This was what we had been preparing for, for so
long. This was *our* place; these were *our* people, *our* responsibility,
and this would be our ministry. It was where God wanted us to be.
Home. Both Audy and I had grown up in mountainous states and felt
very at home with the mountains. Despite the many inconveniences,
we were so excited and content. With the exception of two furloughs,
one year at a new station (Nalja) and six months of teaching on
the eastern half of New Guinea (at the Christian Leaders Training
College), we spent the remainder of our missionary service (about
ten years) at Kiwi.

Like all the other valleys in DNG, it was a beautiful place. Looking
down valley we could see several layers of mountains. One clear day
I counted five ranges fading from dark green to a soft blue in the far
distance.

Rainbows were often seen following an early afternoon rain,
spanning the full width of the valley in brilliant arcs of color—green,
lavender, and yellow being predominant. Sometimes there was a
second bow high upon the mountain sides above the first, larger in
size but softer in its color. Valleys were lush with green vegetation. I
had always loved the mountains in Kentucky. These beautiful displays
of God's creation were very comforting.

Early on, Audy was called "Tuan Dalo" which meant Mr. Big, mostly
because of his size, but also because they considered him a leader.
Sometimes they called him "Father," considering themselves to be his
children. They called me Nonja Dalo, (Mrs. Big), *in spite* of my size.

It was a tremendous privilege and blessing to be a part of seeing God do His work of saving the souls of those from the "back rows" who had previously not been fed. Because God loved them, He sent us and others, to minister to them. We learned to love them with all our hearts. How wonderful it was to see the church emerge and to see leaders step forth, giving their hearts and lives for the service of the Lord.

Other missionaries also spent many years ministering to the Ngalum people at Kiwi. John Greenfield joined us for our first year. Then Ray and Florence Holley stayed for one term (four years). Bill and Judy Carne were at Kiwi about six years. They later spent several years at Mulia. Bill and Laura Fay were at Kiwi about two terms and then had to go home for medical reasons. Finally Jack Hook came. He along with his wife Corky (Coralayne) stayed more than forty years seeing God at work maturing the church.

The Ngalum people are now (2015) able to take over the work themselves, do their own translation, pastor their own churches, and further the ministry in many different ways—even sending out their own missionaries.

Our ministry at Kiwi was covered in my husband's book, *A Missionary's Journal.* After reading the book many people ask me, "What were *you* doing while your husband was doing all that trekking?"

I often answer laughingly, "I was having babies!" That was certainly true the first term. We left America with one little girl and returned four years later with four little girls.

I praise God that I had very few complications with any of my pregnancies even though I had little medical help for the months before delivery. My first delivery, when Beth arrived, was in the hospital in the capital city of Hollandia. Most of the Dutch medical personnel had already returned to Holland because of the threat of war between Holland and Indonesia. (Later, Indonesia took control of the western half of the island of New Guinea.) One Dutch nurse was left, however, and she and a Dutch doctor helped with my delivery.

I stayed in the hospital a few days after Beth's arrival and was cared for by national nurses who walked around barefoot. Geckos, tiny little lizards, crawled around the walls and ceilings. Rice was often served, but with bugs in it! All the rice in the country had bugs, but we always took great pains to get the bugs out before cooking it. Not so at the hospital. The patients had to pick them out themselves. I really liked the Dutch coffee though. It was much like our hot chocolate, very sweet.

Fran (Frances Ruth) was born in a clinic about halfway between the mission vacation house in Sentani and Hollandia in 1961. Some Dutch personnel had returned to the island, and a Dutch midwife was in charge of the clinic. I remember her particularly because she crammed the corner of a blanket in my mouth whenever I made any noise! My delivery took place at night, and she didn't want me to wake other patients. Walls were not soundproof and were open at the top so that the breezes could flow freely.

Fortunately by the time Fran arrived, it was almost time for everyone to wake up, and there was no keeping *her* quiet. Fran was not kept in a nursery, but in a tiny bed attached to the foot of my bed. I loved having her close, especially since the barefoot nurses were always on hand to take care of her.

In a letter to my mother:

"Audy brought Leah and Beth in to see us. They got so excited! Leah asked, "Is this *our* baby? Can we take her home with us?"

When it was time for Alice's arrival, I again went to the hospital in town. A friend was in the hospital also. Audy took a few minutes to visit with him, expecting to hurry right back. But the man prevailed upon him to go get him some ice cream. Audy didn't want to go, but the friend was insistent—apparently very tired of the hospital food. So he went. When he returned Alice had already made her appearance!

Our Mission (UFM) required us to report all pregnancies to the home office. We had informed them when we were expecting Beth and again for Fran. I felt that just a sentence saying, "Well, I'm pregnant again" was boring as well as a bit embarrassing, so when Alice was expected, I decided to write a poem. It follows:

When I looked at my calendar, I realized anew
That our "annual" report is just about due.

We are so happy, it gives us much joy,
Just thinking this time it *might* be a boy!

I mustn't get lengthy lest I be a bore;
Here's the report—we're expecting number four!

We put it into an envelope labeling it "To whom it may concern" and mailed it to headquarters. (Years later, at Alice's wedding, Fran surprised both Alice and me by reading the poem at the reception. She had contacted UFM and found that they still had it in their files.)

❖ ❖ ❖

When we moved to Kiwi we had two children. Leah was about three, and Beth was only a few months old. The people had never seen white children, and both girls were not only white-skinned but had blond hair. People came just to see them and watch them play.

We had a playpen for Beth. A lady whom everyone called "Naning" (grandmother) would come and sit beside the playpen, talking to Beth and keeping her amused for long periods of time. If Beth got tired of being penned up, Naning would happily take her for a walk, carrying her on her shoulders as was their custom. Naning became one of our first believers.

When we returned to Kiwi after our first furlough and a year at a new station, Nalja, we had four little girls running around on the plateau. For a period of time I became very frightened about that eighty-foot precipice dropping down to the river. It ran along the whole left side, not more than a hundred feet from my kitchen door.

One day when Alice was about three years old she asked if she could throw away an old passion fruit. I said "sure," thinking she would throw it in the trash can. But a minute later, I saw her running toward the edge of the cliff. It was too late to yell for her to stop, so I just watched in terror as she ran to the very edge of the cliff, threw the passion fruit over the edge, then turned and came running back, smiling about her accomplishment.

That night I couldn't sleep, I was gripped by fear. How could I keep my children safe when there were these dangerous cliffs all around us? Finally I prayed, "Lord, I can't live here with this fear. Please take it away." Finally I started thinking about all the Scripture I had memorized about fear. "I will fear no evil, for You are with me" (Ps. 23:4). "Do not fear, for I am with you" (Isa. 41:10), and "I sought the Lord, and He answered me, and delivered me from all my fears" (Ps. 34:4).

I pondered these and other Scriptures for a long time, until a great peace came over me. I knew I was where God wanted me to be, so I consciously and willingly placed my children in His hands. He took away my fear and, of course, took care of my children.

Our national friends were always willing to help with the children. They would pull them around in the red wagon sent to us by the folks in our home church, Grace Gospel, or carry them on their shoulders, teaching them their language, or whatever was needed.

They looked out for them also. If someone got hurt, they were quick to pick them up and bring them to me or Audy. However, when Alice and her friend Jonathan Carne were about four and five years old, they decided to go exploring and disappeared. When we started looking for them, asking if anyone had seen them, no one seemed to know where they were. Several people helped us, and we searched the whole plateau, but Alice and Jonathan couldn't be found anywhere. Finally, the tops of their heads appeared from below the plateau. They had gone down the trail to the river and back again! No one had seen them go. We praised God they were all right, but both Jonathan's parents, Bill and Judy Carne, and Audy and I sternly admonished them never again to leave the plateau without permission or without someone older with them!

❖ ❖ ❖

Another incident happened when Leah was about five and Beth was three. When I went in to put them to bed one night, Leah said she didn't want to sleep in her bed but wanted to sleep with Beth. I said, "No, you just stay in your bed, you'll sleep better." But she was insistent that she wanted to sleep with Beth. Finally, I said, "Well, if it's okay with Beth, you can sleep with her." Beth agreed and moved over to make room for Leah.

The next morning when I went in to wake them, I stood wide-eyed and in shock looking at Leah's bed. The entrance to the attic was directly above her bed. It had a door which we had believed was fastened securely. We never dreamed that it could somehow break loose and fall. This door was made of wood and quite heavy, and it was now on Leah's bed! Had she slept in her bed that night, she would have at least had some broken bones, maybe worse.

How we praised God that He put the desire in her heart to sleep with Beth that night. He had once again proven that He would take care of our children. We moved the beds that very day, in addition to repairing the door.

While we "station-sat" at Nalja for a year, our girls learned a valuable lesson. Leah (about six), Beth (four) and Fran (three) decided to take a walk, taking Bobby, our dog, with them. They went out the path from our house and down the airstrip. Seeing an interesting path leading off the airstrip, they decided to see what adventure it might offer. They had gone but a little way when they came to an intersection. Choosing one of the paths, they continued on but soon came to another intersection. After making several turns, they began wondering if they should turn back lest they not be able to retrace their steps.

They started to return home but found that they had already forgotten how to get back to the airstrip. Thoroughly frightened already, their plight became worse when they saw a pig coming up one of the paths. Beth began to cry. Bobby chased the pig away, but Beth still cried.

"Don't cry, Beth," Leah said, "Let's pray and ask God to show us which way to go."

So they prayed, and when they opened their eyes Leah said, "Let's try this way." Sure enough, they were soon in sight of the airstrip and were home in a few minutes. They came in all talking at once, excitedly telling us how God had helped them find their way home.

How happy we were that our girls were learning to trust God. What a picture of how all of us sometimes stray away from our heavenly Father, seeking some worldly adventure. Satan comes along making the situation worse. But God will always show us the way "home" when we ask Him.

We tried to teach our girls that after being put to bed, there should be no talking or calling to us. But when Beth was about five and supposed to be quiet, she called,

"Mommie, what is Kitok's girl's name?" I went to her door.

"Oknangul," I said, "But you know . . ."

She interrupted with, "Do you know why I asked? I'm praying quietly, and I wanted to pray for her." How could I scold her after that?

"Okay, Honey," I said, and returned to my bedroom, thanking God that she was learning to pray for her friends.

On a lighter note, one morning Audy started to have our devotions at the breakfast table. He had read a few verses from the Bible when one of the girls got the giggles. Soon another girl started to giggle. Audy told them to stop being silly as we were reading the Word of God. But soon all the girls were trying to stifle their giggles. Finally I *too* was overcome. That was too much! Audy just closed his Bible. "We'll have devotions at lunch today," he said, trying not to smile too broadly himself.

Medical Work

The medical work I did included some yaws, a tropical disease similar to leprosy. It was easily cured with only a few injections of oil-based penicillin. Malaria was rare. There were the occasional burns, colds, pneumonia, and cuts and bruises. When a storage building was erected at the top of the air strip (several months after our arrival), an area was included to be used as a clinic. Until that time, however, I did all the medical work from my kitchen door.

My medical knowledge was very limited, but the Kiwi people had no one else. I prayed constantly for God's guidance. Audy learned to give the injections for yaws and to do other simple procedures, and he did all he could for sick ones he met while on trek.

The houses at Kiwi were built similar to those at Mulia—one-room, round houses built with poles and slats, fastened together by wrapping with a certain vine. Clay was used to form the round pits in the middle of the room for the fire, and the family slept on the floor around this fire pit. (There was no second floor like the ones at Mulia.) Far too often, someone rolled over into the fire in the middle of the night and got burned.

Once I was dressing the burned hand of a child, perhaps three years old, who had somehow gotten his hand into the fire. I was concerned about keeping the fingers separate in order to give him maximum use of the hand after it healed. I was carefully inserting coated gauze between the fingers. Painful as I'm sure it was, the child was handling it well, only whimpering occasionally. Suddenly there was a loud thump. The mother had passed out and hit the floor! After that, I learned to pay more attention to the mother and have her sit down where she couldn't see the procedures being done on her child.

Another bad burn I tended was on a girl who had been deliberately tied too close to the fire as a punishment. Her knee was badly burned and infected. I didn't think I could do what needed to be done for her, so I called one of the mission doctors by radio, asking if I could send her to him. "No," he said, "You can do it. I'll tell you what to do, and you do it!" I did, but it stretched me way beyond what I was taught in nursing school. The girl recovered, but it was too late to restore full motion to her knee.

I tell the story of stitching a wound for the first time in a letter to my sister:

> Today my houseboy got cut on a rock—I never did get it straight if he fell or if someone threw the rock—they get so excited and jabber so fast! Anyway, it was a good-sized

cut and just above the eye. I had him hold ice on the area for quite a long time, then I put three stitches in it—with a regular needle and thread! I had never done anything like that before, but there's no one else to do it, and I couldn't figure out any other way to close the wound. I gave him some penicillin also, so I hope it heals okay.

It did heal with only a very slight scar. Later I got some proper needles and "thread."

I learned early to listen to the mothers. One mother came saying her child was very sick and described the symptoms of pneumonia. Yet when I examined the child he didn't seem that sick. After some deliberation, I decided to go ahead and treat it as pneumonia in spite of my misgivings, choosing to believe the mother. She didn't return though I had urged her to come back the next day. Later I learned the baby had died. I thanked God that I had done the right thing, and if the mother had come back for further treatment, the child may have lived. Cases like these were heartbreaking when the parents didn't follow through with treatment.

From a letter to my mother:

We are having a flu epidemic, and I've had a time getting folks to come in for treatment. They believe that the flu and many other sicknesses are caused by evil spirits and are afraid of angering the spirits if they accept a "shot." A few have come regularly and have recovered nicely.

It was very hard to get anyone to come several days in a row to get antibiotic injections. Pills and syrups were not yet available.

As soon as the patient improved a little, they quit coming. This happened with another mother who brought her young child to me with pneumonia. She waited much too long to come back, and when she did, I knew as soon as I examined the little girl that nothing was going to help her now. While the mother sat on my kitchen floor holding her sick child, I prepared some medicine knowing it was too late to have any effect.

Before I had the chance to administer the medicine, the child's breathing became even more labored. The mother then started crying and wailing, "My baby is dying! My baby is dying!" There was nothing I could do but cry with her and pray for God's comfort. It was the first time I had seen anyone die, and the fact that it was a child was hard to handle. I determined to keep trying in every way I could to educate these—my—people about caring for their sick.

Eventually we decided to build a "sick hut." A replica of their huts in the village, though quite a bit larger, was erected in my garden area. People who needed longer-term care could come with their families and stay there until treatment was completed. It helped. Still, when the sick person got better, they too often went home before they were well enough.

From a letter to my mother:

> I've had quite a few sick folks lately, so I have been glad for the sick house. One man was there for about four days, then a woman for two days. A baby had a bad case of pneumonia. I kept thinking every day that he would die. I think the mother did too. But she stayed, and we kept up the treatment and kept praying, and he recovered. PTL!

Once a man was carried to the sick hut from down valley—a long trip. Like the man in Scripture who was lowered through the roof by his friends, relatives and friends together carried him to find help. He had some very bad injuries, which had gotten infected. I treated him for several days, and he healed up nicely and went home. About two months later, he appeared at the station along with several friends, carrying what seemed to be a very heavy load. He put it down in front of me and, with a big broad grin, said that he had brought me some pig. In the bag was almost half a pig! I was very touched, and we enjoyed several nice pork meals. Few paid me so handsomely.

There were some things I wouldn't attempt. I never offered to help women with having their babies. Many of the other missionary nurses who had much more training did help with deliveries. But I felt that their methods, which undoubtedly could be improved upon, were adequate much of the time. I feared my lack of knowledge might only make matters worse.

I didn't do any dental work either, except to occasionally give antibiotics for an infected tooth. But one day a man came in with an extremely painful tooth and begged Audy to pull it. Finally Audy decided to try. He had heard of other missionaries who used ordinary pliers to pull teeth. So he tried, but it didn't come out easily, and the man was in such pain. Finally the tooth just crumbled. Austin was dripping with sweat. He felt so bad that he hadn't been able to get the tooth out.

I gave the man something for the pain and antibiotics and he went home. The next day he returned, smiling and happy. The pain was gone. And in a few days the tooth area had healed. But after that

Austin steadfastly refused to try any more dental work. Praise the Lord, a few years later God sent us a dental assistant who knew how to do dental work properly!

❖ ❖ ❖

Sometimes I needed to treat my own family—and even myself. If I needed antibiotics, I simply gritted my teeth and stabbed the front of my thigh. But once after not feeling well for several weeks, I decided to go to the hospital in Hollandia (the capital city—it has a different name now). I was in a ward with several other ladies who were all Dutch. I could not speak Dutch and only one of them could speak enough English for a conversation.

This very attractive young lady was there because of being in a plane crash in which she sustained a broken leg. Since she wasn't sick, she had too much energy for staying in bed all day. So she kept us all entertained with her constant talking and laughing. She was also very helpful in translating what the nurses said to me.

One day out of the blue, she asked, "Lorrie, what is your fate?" At first I didn't realize what she was saying until I remembered that Dutch people have trouble pronouncing the 'th' sound. Then she said, "You know, are you Catholic, or Protestant, or what?" What a wonderful opening! We talked for a while, and then she told me this story.

"My friends and I were on the beach drinking and having a good time. The sun was shining brightly with not even a dark cloud anywhere. We started talking about religion, and I looked up into the sky and yelled, 'Okay, if there is a God, let it be pouring rain in ten minutes!' We all laughed derisively. But in less than ten minutes it was pouring rain! What do you think about that?"

I told her I believed God had given her an answer. I urged her to believe Him and to ask Him into her life. We talked a long time, and

I prayed with her. We were in the hospital together a whole week, and though we talked several times, she didn't make a decision to accept Jesus as her Savior. I hope she did later, and I hope to see her in Heaven. I have prayed for her many times over the years.

It turned out that I had an iron and vitamin deficiency—too many babies and not enough fresh vegetables. I recovered quickly with better nutrition and rest.

A No Rest Vacation

Audy, Alice and I went out to the coast for vacation and to visit the girls at school when Fran was in first grade. All the girls seemed fine, but when we saw the school nurse, she told us that Fran had been very sick and one evening had even been "out of her head." Many of the children, including Fran, had measles and this was a complication. That evening the school staff decided that if she wasn't better by morning, they would call us by radio and take her inland to a doctor.

She *was* better the next morning, and we were supposed to come out in a few days, so they decided to wait until we got there to tell us. Whew! This was hard to hear. We felt so bad that we hadn't been with her when she was so sick but were thankful that now she was much better.

That was just the beginning. That very first night, Alice was playing with a dog when suddenly he whipped around and bit her on the lip! It wasn't a serious bite, but we had it checked out, put ice on it, etc, and it healed just fine. Soon, one by one Leah, Beth and Alice started getting sick with flu-like symptoms, which turned out to be measles.

Leah had the worst case with a high temperature and continual vomiting. She couldn't keep anything down. After several days, she said she thought she could eat a banana. I didn't have any, but I went to all the neighbors, most of them also missionaries, until I found some. She ate one banana, kept it down, and finally started getting better. She missed almost two weeks of school and looked very thin.

As the girls began to get better, Audy and I got sick with colds, though his case was much milder than mine, and he was getting better by the time I became ill. We finally all recovered just about when it was time to go back inland. I wrote to my mother, "I took a whole stack of letters with me to answer while we were on vacation, and didn't write one letter! It sure wasn't a vacation either. I came home exhausted!"

Other Ministries

"Whatever you do in word or deed, do all in the name of
the Lord Jesus, giving thanks through Him to God the
Father."

COLOSSIANS 3:17

More answers to the question. "What were you doing while
Audy was doing all that trekking?"

In the beginning I helped with the literacy program. Our first
primers were made with simple words and short sentences. Our
students, mostly teenage boys, seemed to learn fairly quickly. But we
soon realized that some of them were simply memorizing each page
and reciting it. The concept of having written words on a page (or a
slate), representing objects like trees or bananas was entirely new to
them. But they got the idea eventually.

When other missionaries came to help us, I turned the literacy
program over to their more capable hands. Many missionaries over
a period of years, as well as some Indonesian teachers, helped the
Ngalum people become literate.

I also taught the women. As soon as I knew a little of the language, I started a Bible class. Things progressed slowly. I didn't have much time in the early years, and I struggled with being able to express things in their language, though it did help me in learning the language and in getting to know some of the ladies. At least it laid a foundation for future teaching from God's word. A few years later, after the girls were all in school and I knew the language better, I felt I was making better progress in getting across the truths they needed to learn.

Florence Holley, Judy Carne, and Laura Fay also taught the women, but it was Corky Hook who, over a period of many years, made the real progress, developing Sunday school teachers, Awana leaders, and other helpers in the ministry.

Cooking was always "from scratch," except when someone from home sent us mixes. Recipes often required substitutions. We tried to use native food as much as possible, and all of us developed recipes for a variety of tasty dishes. I, therefore, compiled a cook book. I asked all the other missionary ladies to send me their best recipes, and I put them all together. In those days there was no running off copies from a printer, but we did have slower ways of making extra copies. I made enough copies for most of the missionary ladies in our mission, plus some others. The cookbook was really helpful to all of us, especially in the early years when there was little variety.

In later years, after teaching the national folks how to grow a number of things, we had an abundance of various kinds of fresh vegetables. Tomatoes grew so well that it became a source of income for our people. They began sending them out to the coast for sale at the markets. We also had pineapples, lemons, limes, and lots of bananas. In the lowlands there were papaya, oranges, tangerines, and many other fruits. All of this helped to meet our nutritional needs.

I did a little translation. While Audy was translating five or six books, I translated one—the book of Mark. Of course, all our translations were redone after missionaries became more fluent in the language, and their helpers, informants, became more knowledgeable in the truths of the Bible. But it was a beginning, and each new page of God's Word in their language was received with great joy. It also became an incentive for more people to learn to read. How they loved reading God's Word for themselves!

In the last few years that we were at Kiwi I was able to travel to many of the outstations with my husband. Our national missionaries, especially the women, loved having me come. I helped with the teaching and usually did some medical work.

❖ ❖ ❖

Much of my ministry was to my house help. I have already talked about some of our helpers. They were definitely essential. Without them there would have been little time for language learning or doing ministry. I started out at Kiwi with houseboys. All of the other missionaries on other stations hired boys. However, I began wondering if girls might be better. One day a girl named Tanimkon (pronounced Taaneemkon) appeared at my kitchen door saying she would like to work for me. My decision to hire her was one of the best decisions I ever made.

Tanimkon was very intelligent, willing to work, good with the children, and had an understanding of cleanliness, which none of the boys had. She worked for me for several years. I taught her, and other girls, to iron, fold clothes, make bread and bake cookies as well as to wash dishes, clean parts of the house, and many other things.

Tanimkon also learned many things on her own. While I was learning her language, she learned a bit of mine—to the point that we sometimes had to watch what we said in English in her presence. She often stayed with me when Austin was away, sleeping in the kitchen. She would help me bathe and dress the children for bed and wash the evening dishes.

I found it especially helpful to have her there if one of the children was sick. I particularly remember a time when *I* was sick with a very bad cold. Austin was away, so Tanimkon took care of me and the children very expertly. I was very grateful for her.

We found that our house help often became the first and strongest believers. We had more time with them for teaching and answering questions. Tanimkon was one of the first to ask Jesus to come into her heart and life. Afterward she often went about her work singing the translated version of "Jesus Loves Me" and other songs we had translated into her language and taught to everyone.

Mutki, also one of the early believers and church leaders, became her husband. They had two children and took in one child of a friend who died. (This was a common practice). Mutki helped with the beginning of the work in the Kupel tribe, and many other areas near Kiwi. But he left us all too soon. While we were away from the station for a few weeks, a severe epidemic of influenza went through the valley. Mutki was one of its victims. When we returned, we were so sad to learn that he had died. But, praise God, we knew he was in Heaven.

Kapinip (pronounced Kaapeeneep) was another girl who worked for me. She came along shortly after Tanimkon, and they worked together for a long time. Kapinip wasn't as intelligent, though smart enough. She had very little sense of cleanliness, but she had a wonderful love of life, a great sense of humor, and was willing enough to work. She and Tanimkon worked well together. Kapinip later married Okngungan, who also worked for us. I still used boys to help with the laundry, cut and carry in wood, and many other chores. Okngungan became one of the early leaders of the church, and I believe he was the first pastor of the church on the station.

Okngungan and Kapinip had a rocky marriage for a while. Okngungan liked to go to the dances, and Kapinip was always afraid he would take a second wife while there. It often happened in the Ngalum tribe. We always discouraged taking a second wife as well as attending the dances, but it was a great temptation. Both Kapinip and Okngungan accepted Jesus as their Savior. One day when Okngungan left to go to a dance, Kapinip called after him, "I'm going to be praying for you the whole time you're gone!" He went on to the dance, but her statement kept nagging him, and finally he left the dance and came home. As far as we knew he never went again.

Kapinip had another problem. She was unable to have a child. She had two pregnancies, but both ended in miscarriages. The number one reason why men took second wives was that the first wife failed to have children. One day she confided to me that she was concerned about her situation. So I told her the story of Hannah in the Bible (1 Sam. 1–3) and encouraged her to trust God to give her a child. Then we prayed together.

She, in simple faith, turned her problem over to God. Within a year, God gave them a little girl whom she named Hannah, in honor of the lady who had been an inspiration to her. Later God gave her three other children. After Hannah grew up and married, she and her husband and a younger sister and her husband became missionaries to a tribe in the northern lowlands. This fact makes me want to jump for joy. Praise God for all His blessings.

Tanimkon was the first house girl to have a baby, and she chose to stop working for me at that time. But Kapinip wanted to keep working when Hannah was born. I tried letting her continue, but it soon became evident that it wasn't going to work. I did give her diapers to use for Hannah, though most babies were left naked for the first few years of life. The women placed leaves in the bottom of the large net bags used for carrying babies (or wood or sweet potatoes), and replaced them as needed, but that was as close as they got to diapers. Native babies were never allowed to cry. They were held and fed as needed. I found Kapinip couldn't do much work and still care for her child in the customary way. Reluctantly, I made the rule that after a girl had a baby, she could no longer work in the house.

Kapinip and Okngungan became some of the first Kiwi missionaries to go out to other valleys and help get other works established. This story is told in *A Missionary's Journal*. We had many other helpers and all became our close friends. It was hard to say "good-bye" to them when we returned to the United States.

When the time came that my family and I felt we needed to return home for our children's education, my house help asked lots of questions. Would I have house help in America? How would I cope with all that work and no one to help me? Who would help with the children? They felt so sorry for me when I told them no one would help me. One even offered to go with me, having no idea, of course, how far away that would be or what it would involve.

We did take some of our help with us to the coast a few times. It was difficult for them. Many different languages were spoken there, and even people who may have looked like them, rarely spoke a language they could understand. So many things were new and different. They had never seen cars or trucks or even bicycles, and these things were very frightening, though intriguing.

The ocean, to them, was unbelievable! So much water! We sometimes would go swimming in it. We warned our native friends not to drink the salty water, admonishing, "It will make you sick!" They drank it anyway because they loved the salty taste. I think it was Okngungan who got really sick from ocean water, vomiting all night!

Guests

We actually had quite a lot of company. Friends who lived on the coast enjoyed coming inland to see our work for themselves. Inland missionaries, in addition to going to the coast, also liked to visit other stations. It was a way of learning new ways of doing things and just enjoying being with friends. Audy and I always loved having friends come. And we sometimes went to other stations for part of our vacation time.

Dave and Dina Cole came to visit not too long after we had gotten ourselves settled at Kiwi with their two boys, Larry and Bruce. Larry, and Leah had been playmates at Mulia. But sometimes Leah would shove Larry, and he, being a tiny gentleman, wouldn't shove back. Now he had grown a bit—and as soon as he got off the plane, he walked over to Leah and gave her a big shove. It was like he had decided it was time to pay her back! All four parents burst out laughing. Poor Leah didn't know what was happening, so I quickly picked her up and comforted her. They played together well together after that.

One letter to Mom reads:

We had a family of seven (five children) with us over Christmas, and we had a good time. We had only one big problem—some of the children wet the bed, and we had a time keeping enough sheets and blankets clean and dry since we had wet weather most of the time [of course we didn't have a dryer]. After that, a Dutch couple was "weathered in" for the night.

This happened fairly often. Pilots would start out for the south coast, and the weather would turn bad so that they couldn't cross the central range of mountains. Rather than going back to Sentani (the coast) with a full load, they would drop passengers off at our house. The next day, the pilots would come in with a full load for Kiwi, pick up the folks for the south coast, and continue on. The letter continues:

> A girlfriend of Leah's came for a week; then, after the girls returned to school, we had five men from a mining company stay for nearly a week. Two of them stayed at the Fays'." (This was Bill and Laura Fay who worked with us after Bill and Judy Carne moved to Mulia.)
>
> We really enjoyed having the girls home. In spite of all the company, I think it was one of the best vacations we have had with them. We played games a lot, and trekked out to some villages.

Another letter to Mom:

> Mr. and Mrs. Eden are here. Mr. is a carpenter and helping with the building (an additional house at Kiwi). Mrs. is a helper in everything! She is doing my mending now. [Mrs. Eden helped me bathe and dress the children for bed almost every night, made bread for me, and helped in any way she could. The Edens were in their sixties, so were like grandparents for the girls.]
>
> Ralph Maynard, our field leader, was here last weekend. In about two weeks Mr. Odman (UFM General Director)

and Dr. Brandt are coming and will be coming to Kiwi
first. (They got weathered in—strong winds—and had to
stay two extra days.) Then we'll be going over to Mulia
for some meetings.

While at Mulia, another letter to Mom:

Grandma Eden insisted on keeping Fran (about two years
old) with her at Kiwi so that I could get some rest. So I
left her there. Leah and Beth are busy all day playing with
all the other children. So it has been great for me.

Mrs. Eden helped me in another way also. "Honey, you need to
wear some makeup" she said. I'm naturally very light-skinned. People
often asked me if I felt okay. But in those days wearing makeup was
frowned upon, especially for missionaries. Still, I knew she was right.
I started adding a little artificial color to my face, especially when on
furlough, and people stopped asking how I felt.

Mr. and Mrs. Lehman Keener, who were the first ones to introduce
us to New Guinea, were helping to make a film and spent about two
weeks with us. I was a bit apprehensive at first because Mrs. Keener
had a lot of dietary restrictions. But she made it easy for me, helping
me figure out what she *could* eat, and all was fine. We enjoyed having
them there, and they made a good promotional film for UFM.

Our best visitor was my sister Ivy. She was still single, had been
a nurse midwife in Alaska for several years, and decided to do some
traveling. Unfortunately, she arrived on the coast (Sentani) during a
shortage of airplane fuel, and she had to wait there several days. It

was really hard for all of us to wait, knowing she was so close. Finally she arrived, and we had two great weeks together.

She was with us over Christmas. The day before Christmas we had games and a dinner cooked in the pit with the people. Christmas Day, the Carnes joined us for a big dinner at our house. Ivy had brought gifts for all of us, so it was a great day. Fran's birthday comes only a few days after Christmas, and we had another party for her!

We took Ivy on a fairly long trek, visiting Tanimkon, who had just had her first baby. Ivy gave him a bath, probably the first baby in the tribe to have a bath that young, and patched up some sores on his neck. One of the sores didn't heal, though, so several days later Tanimkon brought him to the station. Ivy lanced the sore, and it finally healed. She gave me lots of good advice for the medical work and left me a few medicines.

Ivy gave everybody hair cuts and gave Judy and me perms. What a treat! It was so good to have family with us. But all too soon it was time for her to return to Alaska.

An Interlude

"Many plans are in a man's heart, But the counsel of the Lord will stand."

PROVERBS 19:21

One of the questions I am often asked is, "Weren't you awfully lonely?"

I *was* lonely at times, but not terribly so. At Kiwi, there were native people around all the time. The schedule of school and all the work around the station continued even when Austin was away. With my children, medical work, and many other things, I was always busy. After the first year, there was another woman on the station most of the time. That helped a lot. The pilots were always willing to take a few minutes to have coffee with us when they came in, unless pressed for time.

For a while we even had a woman pilot. Betty Greene distinguished herself as a pilot during WWII and became one of the founders and leaders of the Missionary Aviation Fellowship. When an extra pilot was temporarily needed in New Guinea, Betty came.

She was such a great lady! I always loved it when she could come to our station and spend time with us. She was always so encouraging and uplifting. It was a great privilege to have known her.

It was while we were at Nalja that I was really lonely. We were virtually all alone there. No other missionaries. Not too many native people came around to visit, and I couldn't speak their language even when they were around. I learned enough to do some medical work, but a lot of communication was in pantomime. Part of the time we brought over some of our house help from Kiwi. Okngungan and Kapinip came, and it was during that time that I told Kapinip about Hannah of the Bible. They were a big help in many ways.

Our year at Nalja came following our first furlough. We had expected to return to Kiwi and were sad to make the change. But Stan and Barb Sadlier, who moved from Ilu only a few months earlier to bring the gospel to that area (called the T valley), needed a furlough. It was not wise to leave such a fledgling work without a missionary, and we were the logical ones to go. Our girls were all under seven and still at home.

The day of my arrival was Beth's fourth birthday. Audy went over the day before, taking Beth and Fran. I brought Leah and Alice. But the Sadliers left on the plane I went in on. Audy had only one day with them, and I had only a few minutes. This was a different tribe and a new language. We knew it was not going to be an easy task.

The Sadliers had built a house, but hadn't been able to do much finishing work.

I kept a diary while at Nalja; some excerpts follow:

Only the kitchen floor was nailed down. It had a smooth finish but had not been varnished. It got dirty very easily. The rest was rough pit-sawn planks, uneven and only nailed down in spots. Sometimes when you stepped on one end, the other end went up a little, and of course, made a bang when it went down again. Often when the planks went up they banged against the aluminum which was used for partitions. The noise was very irritating. Other walls were only heavy paper.

The bathroom was an outhouse with burlap bags for sides. It had a leaky grass roof but had a pretty blue seat from a real commode! The house had real windows (louvers) and running water—from a plastic pipe coming from drums near the roof outside. And there was a shower. There were only two bedrooms, but there was a small study with a door (easier to keep the children out of important papers and language files). I did a lot of standing, looking, and thinking. And then a lot of sewing and fixing. The result was a bright red, white, and blue kitchen, and great improvements in other parts of the house. That lifted my spirits tremendously.

We were short of supplies for the first few weeks. We had very little sugar, so I used it very sparingly. Finally, Pilot Bob Johansen came in with a load of supplies. "Did you bring me some sugar, Bob? This is all I have." I said, showing him my almost empty sugar bowl.

"Humm, There was a large bag, but I think it was rice."

I was terribly disappointed. Bob felt bad too and would only take a tiny bit for his tea. But after he left we discovered it was sugar, 220 pounds of it!

The Sadliers gave us permission to use their washing machine until ours came. But after about three weeks, the fan belt broke. Audy tried in vain to fix it, so we were forced to go back to washing by hand. Okngungan and

Kapinip weren't too happy about that. The day they left to
return to Kiwi, ours arrived. I was so thankful that I didn't
have to wash by hand with no one to help me.

Then the radio died. We did have a receiver, so we could
hear Ralph and others trying to get parts for us. Finally,
after about two weeks, we got a new generator, got the
dead battery recharged, and were on the air again.

But in spite of all the difficulties, as week followed week, we
began thanking God that He had assigned us to Nalja. After a
hectic furlough, the quietness was a most welcome change. It had
a stabilizing effect on us all. We thoroughly enjoyed our family. We
had many good times of playing, talking, and praying together. And
some great things happened.

Leah came to me while I was making a bed. "Mom," she said,
"Did you know that I was saved when we were in America?"

"No," I said, "I didn't know that you were. When was it?"

"Well, do you remember when I asked you how to be saved and
you told me how?"

"Was it then?"

"Uh-huh." She said. "Don't you remember that I told you that
every night I asked Jesus to come into my heart?"

I remembered very well. There had been a period of about two or
three weeks when she had asked all kinds of questions about spiritual
things. "Why did my Sunday school teacher say that she had two
fathers?" "How do people get saved?" We had not wanted to push
or persuade. A decision made on her own, we felt, would be more
sure. So we had simply answered her questions. I had explained that
if you really mean it, you only need to ask Jesus once to save you.

But that day after talking to her further, she seemed to understand fully, and I felt that her salvation was real. It was a time of rejoicing!

Later that same day she and Beth came out of the bedroom holding hands and announcing that Beth had prayed and asked Jesus to come into her heart too! A few weeks later:

We have been reading from a book by Donald Grey Barnhouse each day at breakfast. For a few days the portions from the book were about the contrast between heaven and hell. Audy tried to explain about both in a way that their young minds could understand. Later when the girls were outside playing, they started talking about heaven and hell. Fran, who was only about three years old, started crying and said, "I don't want to go to that bad place where people cry and fuss all the time!" So Leah and Beth brought her in to talk to me. The result was that Fran too asked Jesus to come into her heart and save her.

That left only Alice. After we returned to Kiwi, and again after reading the Bible at breakfast, she said, "I'm always wanting to get saved, but I never get saved!" So she also made the decision to ask Jesus to save her. They were only children, but all of them proved as they grew older that those decisions were real and firm.

❖ ❖ ❖

We decided to send the Kiwi house help home, hoping to be able to hire some of the Nalja young people. But we couldn't persuade anyone to do the job. I found that I was doing most of the work and getting very tired. Audy helped as much as he could, but he had other work to do—work on the language, the air strip, and many other things. There was also a lot of stealing which he felt he needed to deal with, lest it become a bigger and bigger problem.

As time went on I began doing more medical work. One afternoon we heard wailing and moaning in a village just up the hill. It kept up for quite a while sounding like someone was hurt or someone had died. I sent a man up to find out. He came back saying a woman had been stabbed several times with a bone dagger for stealing potatoes. Earlier Audy had seen about fifteen men go up to that village. It was just after they left that the wailing began. "Will she die?" we asked. He seemed quite sure that she would not die and would be okay. I didn't know what I should do, not wanting to get involved in their fights. I decided to wait until I was asked before going up.

About a week later the lady's husband came down indicating that she was very sick and wanted me to come. So I collected my medicines and went, taking Leah and Beth with me. It was a steep climb, but once there, the view was magnificent. I was amazed at how well they could watch our activities below. The husband showed us which hut and we crawled along the narrow "hallway" and through the door. There were several people inside. The lady was feverish, but not as bad as I had thought she might be.

It was very dark in the hut. I tried to convey that I needed them to blow up the fire so I could see. They got the point, and the husband also parted the grass of the roof to let in the light. I did as much as I could for her and promised I'd come back tomorrow.

The next day I went back. When I finished with the stabbed lady, they took me to another hut where they said a sick lady lived. When I went in, I saw that she had a large yaws sore on her mouth. I didn't have the proper kind of antibiotic for her, so I decided to try shouting down to Audy. He said he could hear me perfectly. He got a young boy to bring me the medicine, and I gave the lady the injection.

There were about fifteen other huts in that village with a large one in the middle, which had drawings on the sides done with red clay. Probably a spirit house. There was mud everywhere—"dirty" mud where pigs had been. We—Leah and I—managed to make it through the mud and returned home.

About a month later, a little boy asked me to go to the top village; someone was sick. I grabbed my medicines and followed him, taking Leah with me again. The path was wet, muddy, and slippery in places. The last part was straight up. I had to pull Leah up behind me. The sick lady, the mother of our guide, was in the first house.

We peered into the house through the smoke. Leah covered her eyes and didn't want to go in. But it was better inside than at the door, so she came in later. The lady showed me her leg. An arrow had gone completely through her thigh, and both the entrance and exit wounds were infected. I did the best I could for her and we started home. But without our guide we got a bit lost and had to go through some tall grass and mud in order to get back on the right path.

Again, I had to go up several days in a row to treat her wounds and give antibiotic injections. However, I felt it was well worth the effort. All of these women fully recovered, which probably wouldn't have happened without the medicines I was able to use. These trips also helped in gaining the confidence and friendship of the people. They always seemed pleased when I brought the children with me.

Then Audy came down with malaria. I suspected malaria right away and gave him medicine for it, but there are several kinds and several kinds of medicines. Apparently I hadn't used the right kind for this type of malaria. He was really sick with multiple cycles of chilling, fever, and sweating.

I called a doctor by radio. His suggestions didn't work either. After a few days the doctor came over, made a better assessment, and finally, Audy began to get better. He had lost ten pounds. It took him two more weeks to regain his strength. It was quite trying for him having been sick so little during his life.

By the time Audy was recovering, I was exhausted and decided that we had to have some house help. The Coles offered to send Audy's old friend Yamo and his wife, and they proved to be a tremendous help. We didn't know the Dani language very well, but we could manage. Yamo and his wife Giakwe were well-trained and didn't need much instruction. They stayed with us until the Sadliers returned.

We did have several groups of company which temporarily took away the loneliness. In my diary I mentioned that one of the pilots stayed for lunch. That didn't happen often, so we were grateful for his thoughtfulness. We went out a few times just for a break and once for a week of conference. We always enjoyed conference when we could visit with all the other missionaries. The APCM group and the American branch met together, so it was a sizable group. The children had special activities too, which they loved.

There were other bright spots during our year at Nalja:

Today is plane day. Three packages came from Grace Gospel—mostly food, and three packages from Blacksburg, Va. Those folks really outdid themselves. There were clothes, food, and a package of small gifts for each of us. Besides all this, our Australian food order, which we ordered six months ago, came. It arrived in Sukarna Pura [formerly Hollandia, the capital city] in October [this was Feb.] and was that long getting released from customs. Fortunately everything had been packed well and was in good condition.

We oohed, aahed, sampled, tried on, and looked until we
were exhausted. Then we cleaned up and settled down
to read the mail. Great day!

Both Audy and I did a lot of reading in the evenings after getting
the children to bed. It was a great blessing, and we found that our
spiritual lives were deepened through the hardships and the reading.

Today I finished reading Hudson Taylor—both volumes.
Great blessing! I'm asking God to teach me to rest in
Him. (His favorite hymn was "Jesus, I am resting, resting
in the joy of what Thou art") I have so much to learn.

And later I wrote:

I read *Behind the Ranges,* the life story of J. O. Fraser,
pioneer missionary among the tribal people of China. It
was evident that Fraser was a man of prayer. The chapter
on "The prayer of faith" was especially moving. God is
writing messages on my heart, teaching me lessons I
need to learn. I need to spend more time in prayer, then
rest in God for the accomplishment of His will.

I wrote down many Bible verses about prayer:

Mark 11:22–23 Have faith in God (Hudson Taylor
translated it as "Rely on God's faithfulness"). "Truly I

say to you, whoever says to this mountain, 'Be taken up
and cast into the sea,' and does not doubt in his heart,
but believes that what he says is going to happen, it will
be granted him."

Matt. 21:22 "And all things you ask in prayer, believing,
you will receive."

John 15:7, 16 "If you abide in Me, and My words abide
in you, ask whatever you wish, and it will be done
for you. . . . You did not choose Me but I chose you,
and appointed you that you would go and bear fruit,
and that your fruit would remain, so that whatever you
ask of the Father in My name He may give to you."

Jeremiah 32:17 "Ah Lord God! Behold, You have made the
heavens and the earth by Your great power and by Your
outstretched arm! Nothing is too difficult for You."

This one, which is my life verse, Jeremiah. 33:3: "Call to Me and
I will answer you, and I will tell you great and mighty things you
do not know."

There were twenty passages listed, many with several verses. I
studied them all and prayed fervently that God would help me to
make these truths a part of my very being.

At the end of the year the Sadliers returned from furlough, and
we returned to Kiwi. Both Audy and I felt it had been one of the
hardest years of our lives, but in another way, had also been one of
the best. We learned a lot and grew a great deal spiritually. We still
had a long way to go, but I certainly got to know God and His Word
much better. Audy said much the same thing. However, we were

really happy to return to Kiwi. We spent the rest of that term (four years) and our last term (three years) at Kiwi.

That was almost fifty years ago. Today, after other missionaries spent many years of living with and teaching the Nalja people, they are, like Kiwi, on their own. They are doing their own translations of teaching materials and doing their own teaching and preaching. God has done great things in their midst!

–

16

Returning to America

> "Be strong and courageous, do not be afraid or tremble at them, for the Lord your God is the one who goes with you. He will not fail you or forsake you."
>
> DEUTERONOMY 31:6

One of the greatest difficulties a missionary faces is how the children will react to life in a foreign country. How will they handle the culture, the language, and in many cases, separation from parents and siblings for schooling? We were aware of all these situations before going to New Guinea, and we prayed much for guidance from God as we sought to do what was best for our daughters.

Regarding the culture and language, the girls did very well. They adapted to the culture easily—it was what they experienced almost all their early lives. We actually worked in three languages and an extra dialect. Lani, at Mulia; Ngalum at Sibil and Kiwi, with the Sibil dialect being a bit different from Kiwi; and for a short time the Kupel language at Nalja and Yapil. We also studied Indonesian, the National language, but I didn't learn enough to carry on a good conversation. Audy did better than I because he needed to deal with government officials from time to time. The girls learned a bit of the Ngalum language and, at school, a little Indonesian.

Having the children go away to a boarding school was a different story. There were few materials available for home schooling in those days, and the prevailing thought was that children needed to be in a school system where they were educated according to an American curriculum and where there was opportunity to socialize with other American children. Several mission organizations set up boarding schools in several countries for the purpose of educating missionary children. Most missionaries were required to send their children to such a school beginning at first grade.

Our mission did not have their own school and did not make any requirements of us, but another mission's school was available. Thinking it was what was best for them, we hardly even considered keeping our girls at home, although sending them away was very difficult for the whole family. Actually the word "difficult" is a gross understatement. It was heart-rending—one of the hardest things I have ever faced, yet we felt it had to be done.

The mission school was on the coast, about an hour's flight (by Cessna airplane) away from Kiwi. Leah was the first to go to school. We were glad that because her birthday is in November, she didn't need to go until she was almost seven years old. Beth was younger when she went, barely six, and could hardly see out of the airplane window as she waved "good-bye." I smiled and waved until the plane took off, then went down to my house and cried.

A letter to my mother:

Leah and Beth go back to school on Thursday. (Today is Monday). It is quite a job getting them ready. All items of clothing have to have name tags. They seem quite

cheerful about going now, though Leah seemed to dread
it for a while. We've been doing a few special things
this last week, took a short trek and had a picnic on
Saturday, have had ice cream twice. We asked what they
wanted for Sunday dinner and they said "cherry pie and
chocolate ice cream!" What a mixture, but we had it—we
had received some canned cherries from our church in
Huntington (W. Va.), and we have a hand-crank ice cream
maker.

The girls went to school in August and came home for a month
at Christmas and three months in the summer. We tried to plan our
vacations so that we could be with them on the coast for two weeks
each term. Every time a plane came in to Kiwi, we tried to send a
letter to each child, and we sent some kind of gift (often homemade
cookies) as often as we could. Still, there was a lot of time in between
vacations, and they were much too young to be away from family
for months at a time.

There were some rules in place at the school those first years
which made matters worse. For instance, when families came out to
visit, the children were not allowed to stay with their parents. Praise
God that was eventually changed. By the time Fran and Alice went to
school, children could stay with their parents the whole time they were
on the coast—even if it was several weeks. That was so much better!

There were also some more serious problems. Most of the teachers
and house parents were kind and caring, but one or two were not
and cruelly mistreated certain children. Leah and Beth (and others)
have suffered all their lives as a result of some things that were done
to them. The problems continued for the whole time our girls were
in school, though for Fran and Alice to a much lesser degree.

In going through my letters to my mother (she kept them all) I noticed that I often asked for prayer for the girls, but very little was said about problems they were facing at school. That was partly because we didn't want Mom to worry but also because we didn't really know much of what was happening. For a while it seemed that we missed the girls more than they missed us. They seemed to always be doing fun things. Later we learned that their letters to us were "censored," and they were required to write only positive things about their experiences at school. Once in a while, they were able to "smuggle" a more realistic letter to us by finding other ways to get it to the pilots. That was when we began realizing that things were not as we had thought or hoped.

When Leah was in the fifth grade and we were on our second furlough, Audy and I learned more of the difficulties our girls had experienced. We talked with Leah and Beth about possibly not returning to New Guinea for a third term. But Leah said that she wanted to graduate with her class. She preferred to go back in spite of the problems she would face. So we went back, but only for three years. The school only went up to the eighth grade. After that it would have been necessary to send her even farther away. Beth too, would have been ready for high school in another year. For years we had been praying and talking about what we should do when our girls were ready for high school since there was no English-speaking high school in the country.

Even though the full extent of what they had been through did not become evident until we had been home for a while, we knew enough to be aware that we needed to have all our girls at home with us during their high school years. They had already suffered more than enough.

After returning to the United States, little by little, the girls told us more of what they endured at the boarding school, and our hearts ached as we learned what a high price they had paid for us to be able to take the gospel to the Ngalum people. It was a tragedy that should not have happened. We know from experience that God knows all and is the Great Comforter. He can turn tragedy into triumph. All four girls have had some counseling and, praise God, they are all wonderful girls (women), walking with the Lord, and living happy, productive lives.

The boarding situation changed dramatically shortly after we came back to America. Some of the missions who had children at the school built their own hostels where the children received love, care, and adequate supervision and attention in a more home-like atmosphere. The man who had been responsible for most of the abuse did not return after his next furlough. Several years later, he did apologize and ask for forgiveness. That helped considerably.

I'm so glad that mission boards are now more aware of the needs of their missionary kids and have made a lot of changes regarding their educational requirements. Today, in most countries, it is not necessary for children to go to school away from home and certainly not at such a young age. There are many other options available to missionaries such as home schooling, national schools, local missionary schools, and cyber schools.

We were greatly encouraged when, many years later, the mission board involved with the situation in New Guinea did a lot of investigation, apologized for the hurt caused, and has tried to right some of the wrongs that our daughters and others experienced. Still there are many problems in any mission situation, which need love, care, and attention.

❖ ❖ ❖

The plight of our girls was not the only factor that took us home. We had always questioned whether New Guinea would be a lifetime assignment. We had seen the need for more missionaries to join the work in New Guinea and knew that most mission boards were constantly pleading for more help. Audy felt he would like to work on the home end, training, recruiting, and sending out missionaries to the needy countries of the world. And, of course, when it came down to making any decision, the main consideration was always, "What does God want us to do?" We became more and more convinced that God wanted us to make a change. So we made plans to end our ministry in New Guinea after our third term.

For our last six months, our mission gave permission for Audy and me to accept an invitation to go to the Eastern side of New Guinea. The Christian Leaders Training College, near the town of Mt. Hagen in Papua New Guinea, was in temporary need of teachers, and we were asked to help fill that need. The work on that side of the island was much more advanced, and the school was conducted entirely in English. It was a great opportunity.

I was able to teach English and how to use the Bible to teenage Papuans. I enjoyed it immensely. We had vocabulary studies, spelling tests, Bible memorization, and played games which helped them find passages of Scripture quickly. Audy taught evangelism and counseling classes. We both felt we had been able to make important contributions to the training of those students.

Our daughters came over for a weeklong visit about halfway through the semester. All of us loved being together. We did a lot of fun things and visited some shops in the town of Mount Hagan. And Dr. J. O. Sanders played tennis with them. This great man—author, teacher, well-known speaker, and former Director of Oversees Missionary Fellowship (The historic China Inland Mission) was at the college filling in as Guest President. He was so kind to spend time with our children. Audy and I also counted it an exceptional blessing to have been able to get to know this godly man.

Our children returned to school happy to know that it was only for a few weeks, yet sad at the thought of leaving all their friends who had become like brothers and sisters to them. When we finished our assignment at CLTC, we went back across the border, attended Leah's graduation, and then prepared for travel to the United States.

❖ ❖ ❖

It was hard to say "good-bye" to all of the dear friends we had made. Other missionaries were in place at Kiwi to continue the work, however, and nationals were being trained to take on more and more of the ministry themselves. We knew God would guide and help all of them in all of their endeavors as He had helped us.

In every area of our lives and ministry God had proven Himself faithful. He was big enough, kind enough, and wise enough to guide us through all the years in New Guinea. We had done the basics, the beginnings. Now others would carry it further with the help and guidance of this same Great God. As for us, we knew God would be with us as we returned to the United States. Our ministry was not over because the location had changed. God still had work for us to do for Him.

Audy and I were so grateful that God had given us the privilege to serve Him in the beautiful wonderful country of New Guinea.

When Audy took me to Huntington the first time and introduced me to all the pastors, the assistant pastor's wife remarked to her husband, "Oh, I hope he doesn't marry her. . . . She would never make it on the mission field! She's much too pale and small." She told me about her remark several years later, and we laughed about it. But I *had* made it for almost sixteen years because God chooses to use the weak and foolish (1 Cor. 1:27) in order to show His mighty strength. He certainly did that for me.

I wrote the following song expressing how grateful I am that God loved me enough to make me one of His servants. The melody is the familiar, "I Am So Glad That Jesus Loves Me."

I am so glad I surrendered to God,
Followed His leading and proclaimed His Word;
Promised to serve Him eternally;
Oh, what an honor that God uses me.

I am so glad I yielded my all,
Gave Him my life, answered His call.
I am so glad that He uses me,
God uses even me.

What joy to see souls who were lost deep in sin,
Come to the Savior for cleansing within;
Grow in His love and study His Word;
Then become burdened for those who've not heard.

All sacrifices then seem so small;
They're just for a moment and so worth it all.
What a great life! The best that can be!
Praise God, He's using me.

> "Something that has impressed me clearly recently is
> that God is big enough. He is strong enough to help me
> in all my limitations and weaknesses—so why do I need
> to feel inferior or inadequate? He is big enough to control
> or overrule . . . every situation that comes into my life. My
> God is all that I need."
>
> FROM *A MISSIONARY'S JOURNAL* BY AUSTIN LOCKHART

Austin and I found the above statement as true in America as in Irian Jaya (Papua, Indonesia).

After spending a few months visiting family and friends after returning to the States, we moved to South Carolina for Austin to get his master's degree at Columbia Bible College. After finishing his degree, Austin accepted a teaching position at Lancaster Bible College in Lancaster, Pennsylvania.

The culture in Pennsylvania proved foreign to all of us. Our daughters found it very hard to make friends, and greatly missed their friends in Papua. Other children ridiculed them because they knew nothing about the current popular TV shows. Some of Fran's classmates started calling her "Fran Tarkington."

"Who's Fran Tarkington?" she asked.

"Don't you know anything? He's a football player!"

And so it went. Even at church, although people demonstrated more kindness, they waited for our children to put forth the effort to become friends. It took years for them to adjust, and moving so many times only added to the stress. But the difficulties helped them learn to depend on God for all their needs. I am so thankful that all four of them dedicated their lives to serve God in any way He should lead.

Austin taught missions at Lancaster Bible College for five years, and then we moved to Langhorne, Pennsylvania, where we worked with Biblical Ministries Worldwide for another five years. Austin traveled a lot during those years, supervising missionaries in Europe and Asia.

Then the call came to resurrect a small mission that almost faded away. This time we moved to Lebanon, Pennsylvania. We stayed there for thirteen years, eleven of which Austin worked as the General Director of Gospel Furthering Fellowship.

Three of our girls married Pennsylvanians. We loved them all. After graduating from Philadelphia Bible College, Fran moved to Texas to find a job, married a wonderful Texan, and never came back.

Today, Leah and her husband run a thriving stamp business. They volunteer at their church as time and schedules permit. Beth and her husband served as missionaries in South Africa for eighteen years. Today Beth works as a counselor on staff at her church, and her husband teaches at Lancaster Bible College. Fran lost her first husband to brain cancer, after which she published *Widowed: When Death Sucks the life out of You*, a book she wrote to help widows. She and her second husband started a publishing ministry near Dallas, Authenticity Book House, focusing particularly on study helps for pastors and teachers in other countries. Alice had a music ministry (singing) for a number of years, but now she works as an executive secretary in the special needs department of the Philadelphia area schools. Both she and her husband serve their local church in music and sound.

In 1988, God gave us two more daughters—teenagers. Following the death of my oldest sister, her daughters came to live with us. After enduring so much heartache, Becky and Paula grew into wonderful and beautiful women I love dearly.

When the opportunity arose for Austin and me to teach at Southland Bible Institute, we moved to Ashland, Kentucky. I taught a few courses, and Austin came alive with the opportunity to teach missions again. Even before leaving Pennsylvania, Audy began experiencing health problems, and in 2006 the Lord called him home to Glory.

This is a very "bare bones" sketch of our lives. Over the years, we endured many trials, heartaches, and losses, but we also experienced many blessings, joys, and victories. We especially enjoyed seeing young people dedicate their lives to the Lord and serve Him all around the world.

What rejoicing there will be when we see our Savior face to face and meet the ones who accepted Christ as a result of our dedication to Him. Audy gets to experience this already.

Today I live in Pennsylvania near most of my daughters. Living alone imposed a very different life on me, but again, God proves himself great and still remains BIG enough to meet my every need.

How to Surrender to Christ

"Jesus said, 'I am the way, and the truth, and the life. No one comes to the Father except through me.'"

JOHN 14:6

"But as many as received Him, to them He gave the right to become children of God."

JOHN 1:12

'm so glad that I found Jesus when I was young. I have had a wonderful life living with Jesus and serving Him. He has been with me through all the good times and the bad, even when the bad was as horrendous as a rape. God was my helper and comforter through it all.

Jesus invites us all to know Him. We must simply accept his gift of eternal life by believing Jesus died on the cross for our sins. Ask God to forgive you. If you believe Jesus died on the cross for your sins, take a minute to pray and surrender your life to God. Ask Him to help you follow Jesus. Know that God's not mad at you. He loves you and waits ready to embrace you in his grace and freedom.

What's Next?

- Know Christ makes us a new creation. "Therefore, if anyone is in Christ, he is a new creation. The old has passed away; behold, the new has come" (2 Cor. 5:17, ESV).

- God forgives our sins and allows us a new start. "Blessed are those whose lawless deeds are forgiven, and whose sins are covered" (Rom. 4:7, ESV).

- He grants us eternal life. "For God so loved the world, that he gave his only Son, that whoever believes in Him should not perish but have eternal life" (John 3:16, ESV).

- God gives us indescribable joy. "Though you have not seen Him, you love him. Though you do not now see him, you believe in him and rejoice with joy that is inexpressible and filled with glory, obtaining the outcome of your faith, the salvation of your souls" (1 Pet. 1:8–9, ESV).

- We begin talking to God about all aspects of our life. We ask Him to show us which paths to take or what decisions to make, and we start communicating to Him even the tiny details of our lives. But let's not forget to listen. God wants to speak back.

- God talks to us through the Bible, so start reading his message to you. Websites such as BibleGateway.com or YouVersion.com offer a variety of translations free of charge.

We recommend beginning with the Gospel of John or one of the other Gospels to learn what Jesus taught during His time on earth.

✤ Lastly, Authenticity Book House would love to hear about your decision to follow Christ. E-mail us at info@abh-books.com. We would love to pray for you and celebrate the new life you have in Christ.

About the Author

Lorrie Lockhart was born in rural Kentucky to loving parents who knew very little about God. Through missionaries, she found God and learned that, though small in stature, God could use her. At a young age, Lorrie felt God drawing her into missions. She and her husband Austin spent many years on the island of New Guinea teaching primitive tribes about God's love and redemption. Lorrie now lives in Pennsylvania near most of her grown daughters and enjoys spending time with her family and in the ministry of prayer.

The Ministry of ABH

Authenticity Book House is a nonprofit publishing ministry that:

- Serves gifted Christian authors by removing publishing barriers.
- Equips non-English speaking pastors and teachers with biblical literature in their heart languages.
- Employs skilled believers in developing nations.

Serving Aspiring Authors

- Authors own all copyrights.
- ABH absorbs all costs for cover design, editing, formatting, proofreading, translating, and marketing of the author's first three books.
- ABH does not take any royalties on sales of the author's first three books.

Equipping Pastors Worldwide

- 20 percent of net royalties on all ABH books goes to support international pastors.
- ABH targets strategic language groups that lack biblical resources.

Empowering Believers

- ABH selects authors with confirmed Christlike character and ministry effectiveness.
- ABH employs translators and editors around the globe.

Please help us glorify Christ in editorial excellence. If you find a mistake in this book, please e-mail the error and the page number to quality@abhbooks.com.